People at the Top of the Charts

Rock Stars

People at the Top of the Charts

ANDREW DAVID

Exeter Books

NEW YORK

1988
$5.00

Cover Design: joe mistak
Book Design: muriel underwood
Production Coordinator: ruth guest
Editorial Director: jim hargrove

Special thanks also to Ray Levin for his valuable suggestions for groups to be included in this book.

ROCK STARS: People at the Top of the Charts
Copyright © 1979 by Quality Books, Inc.
An Exeter Book
Distributed by Bookthrift, Inc.
New York, New York

ISBN 0-89673-034-4

1 2 3 4 5 6 7 8 9 10

Manufactured in the United States of America.

Contents

Introduction	7	Kansas	52
Performers (in alphabetical order)		Carole King	54
Aerosmith	12	Kiss	56
The Bee Gees	14	Barry Manilow	58
Boston	16	Paul McCartney & Wings	60
Jackson Browne	18	Olivia Newton-John	62
The Captain & Tennille	20	The Rolling Stones	64
Chicago	22	Linda Ronstadt	66
Eric Clapton	24	Todd Rundgren	68
The Commodores	26	Santana	70
Alice Cooper	28	Bob Seger & the Silver Bullet Band	72
Neil Diamond	30	Carly Simon	74
The Doobie Brothers	32	Cat Stevens	76
Earth, Wind & Fire	34	Rod Stewart	78
Emerson, Lake & Palmer	36	Barbra Streisand	80
Fleetwood Mac	38	Styx	82
Foreigner	40	Jethro Tull	84
Peter Frampton	42	The Who	86
Aretha Franklin	44	Stevie Wonder	88
Andy Gibb	46	Yes	90
Billy Joel	48	Index	95
Elton John	50		

Introduction

Back in 1958, the year the Record Industry Association of America (RIAA) first got around to awarding gold records, people just weren't buying records like they would in the late 1070s. Only four singles that year sold a million copies: Perry Como's *Catch a Falling Star, Patricia* by Perez Prado, Laurie London's *He's Got the Whole World in His Hands,* and Rock's only entry, *Hard Headed Woman,* from the throat and guitar of the now lionized Elvis Presley. The only album certified gold that year was the movie soundtrack of the Rodgers and Hammerstein musical *Oklahoma.*

In the early months of 1979, times were very different. When the RIAA announced its certifications for the preceding year, this time it was a record-setting 193 gold albums and 61 gold singles. And beyond that, 102 albums and 10 singles earned platinum certification (twice the total sales needed for gold), a new ultimate category introduced in 1976. It could be said in 1979, too, that a person would be hard-pressed to find among the golds and platinum a record that could not be classified in the genres of Pop/Rock or Rhythm & Blues. Almost anyway — there were 15 or 20 Country music records in there among them, contributed by the likes of Willie Nelson, Waylon Jennings, and Dolly Parton; and a few of Steve Martin's comedy routines; and the soundtrack from *Close Encounters of the Third Kind.* But that was about all.

In the music world, 1958 was a landmark year for another reason, too. It was also the year that the National Academy of Recording Arts and Sciences (NARAS) was founded. The purposes of this illustrious group were manyfold; all of them, however, were aimed at advancing the cause of what had become one of the entertainment world's most potent mediums, recorded sound. To encourage and reward quality, NARAS instituted the Grammy Awards, little gold victrolas to be awarded annually to the top performers and their products, which in a very short time would assume the same stature in the recording arts industry as the Oscar, the Emmy, and the Tony would in their fields of entertainment. And so in 1958 the first Grammies were given out. The award for Record of the Year was won by *Nel Blu Dipinto Di Blue,* better known as *Volare,* by Domenico Modugno, and the first Album of the Year so honored with a Grammy was Henry Mancini's *The Music from Peter Gunn.*

In the more than 20 years since top-selling records have been honored with precious metal discs and performers have been acknowledged with Grammy awards, popular music has changed considerably. So have the musical tastes and buying habits of the listening public. Some performers have stood the test of time, but in most cases the faces and forms have come and gone. Individuals have died, fallen from favor, passed into obscurity. Groups have soared to the top of the Charts, only to dwindle away or disband later. Sudden stars, male and female alike, have shimmered under the

Gold and Platinum Records

Official certification of gold and platinum records is awarded by the Record Institute Association of America (RIAA) in New York City. The basic requirements are:

Platinum album — Sales of 1 million copies
Platinum single — Sales of 2 million copies
Gold album — Sales of 500,000 copies
Gold single — Sales of 1 million copies

Only sales in the United States are tallied for official certification, and no promotional copies, record club bonuses or dividends, or other records distributed without charge can be counted. At least 50% of the record's sales must go through regular retail channels.

Scorecard
A comparative look at who has won the most of what among the 40 Pop/Rock performers featured in this book.

Platinum Albums

Kiss — 5
Neil Diamond — 4
Barry Manilow — 4
Paul McCartney & Wings — 4
Linda Ronstadt — 4
Barbra Streisand — 4

Platinum Singles

The Bee Gees — 2
Andy Gibb — 1
Olivia Newton-John — 1

Gold Albums

The Rolling Stones — 22
Barbra Streisand — 22
Elton John — 15
Neil Diamond — 13
Chicago — 12
Santana — 12
Jethro Tull — 12
Eric Clapton — 11
Paul McCartney & Wings — 10

Gold Singles

Aretha Franklin — 13
Elton John — 10
The Bee Gees — 9
Olivia Newton-John — 8
Paul McCartney & Wings — 7
Captain & Tennille — 5
Neil Diamond — 5
Barry Manilow — 5
The Rolling Stones — 5

Grammy Awards

Stevie Wonder — 14
Aretha Franklin — 10
Barbra Streisand — 6
The Bee Gees — 5
Earth, Wind & Fire — 4
Carole King — 4
Paul McCartney & Wings — 4
Olivia Newton-John — 3

momentary clamor of international attention and instant recognition, only to see it fade away almost as fast as it came. Rhythm and blues, heavy metal, soul, hard rock, soft rock, acid rock, punk rock, reggae, disco, all of them have been part of the contemporary musical scene at one time or another during those years. It has been an exciting, fulfilling period in the history of music.

The Rock scene began back in the early and mid 1950s — no one can really pinpoint exactly when. But it was somewhere around the time that the Charts — as they existed in those days — began losing names like Tony Martin, Tony Bennett, and Frankie Laine; Teresa Brewer, Rosemary Clooney, and Patti Paige; the Ink Spots, the Andrews Sisters and eventually even Mitch Miller. It was that time when the public suddenly began listening to (and buying the records of) Bill Haley and the Comets, Buddy Holly, Little Richard, Fats Domino, Jerry Lee Lewis, the Everly Brothers, and of course Ray Charles and Elvis Presley.

Rock did not, however, replace the more conventional music of the 40s and early 50s overnight. In fact, quite the opposite, it was not until well into the 1960s that the Charts and the RIAA certifications began to recognize the new wave of Rock and Pop. Until 1964 the Charts were still dominated by names like Mantovani, Ray Coniff, Percy Faith, Harry Belafonte, Andy Williams, and the Kingston Trio. Elvis was the only Rock entertainer who could claim a place in the superstardom of that era, his was the only Rock name that consistently showed up on the Charts and whose records chalked up top sales. But things in the music world were in a state of change, one that would prove to be irreversible.

By 1964, the transformation had pretty much taken place. The Pop of Barbra Streisand and the Rock of the Beatles had established a proverbial foothold in the contemporary musical theater of operations. Suddenly there were new names commanding attention like the Beach Boys, the Rolling Stones, the Supremes, Herman's

Major Grammy Awards for 1978
(Awarded in March 1979)

Record of the Year: Billy Joel, *Just the Way You Are*

Album of the Year: The Bee Gees, *Saturday Night Fever*

Song of the Year: Billy Joel, *Just the Way You Are*

Best Pop Vocal Performance, Female: Anne Murray, *You Needed Me*

Best Pop Vocal Performance, Male: Barry Manilow, *Copacabana*

Best Pop Vocal Performance, Group: The Bee Gees, *Saturday Night Fever*

Best New Artist of the Year: A Taste of Honey

Hermits, Bob Dylan, and a host of others.

NARAS had been as cautious in accepting Rock and Roll as the general public had. The organization did not bestow a Grammy on a Rock performer or a Rock record until 1964 when they granted the Beatles the honor of being the Best New Artist of the Year and awarded them another Grammy for their rendition of *A Hard Day's Night* as the Best Pop Vocal Performance by a Group. It was a start, but Rock musicians and their products would not, however, dominate the Grammy awards until the 1970s.

As the 1960s wore on, Aretha Franklin made her debut and was instantly acknowledged as the Queen of Rhythm and Blues. The Grateful Dead appeared at one end of the Rock spectrum and we found the Monkees at the other end of it. Somewhere in between, there was Paul Revere and the Raiders, The Doors, Englebert Humperdinck, Otis Redding, Cream, the Fifth Dimension, and a variety of other lesser-knowns.

The end of the 1960s and the beginnings of the 1970s brought Rock into the world of the musical drama and the opera. *Hair* was an overwhelming smash; it was followed effectively by *Tommy, Jesus Christ Superstar,* and *Godspell,* and the one-time compartmentalized world of Rock took on a worldly and artistically appreciated significance.

The years of this decade, the 1970s — at least in the Rock world — belong to the 40 subjects of this book. They have been the superstars, and all 40 of them still are today. There were others, too —some of them are gone now, others still here, but their contributions during the last 10 years have been very substantial: Roberta Flack, the Carpenters, Blood, Sweat & Tears, Sonny & Cher, Three Dog Night, the Moody Blues, Credence Clearwater Revival, Janis Joplin, Led Zeppelin, Sly & the Family Stone, Joe Cocker, Jimi Hendrix, the Allman Brothers, Gladys Knight & the Pips, Bette Midler, Neil Young, The Association, Kris Kristoferson, Helen Reddy, John

Billboard Magazine Awards for 1978

Top Pop Male Artists

1. *Andy Gibb*
2. *Barry Manilow*
3. *Billy Joel*
4. *Shaun Cassidy*
5. *Chuck Mangione*
6. *Eric Clapton*
7. *Rod Stewart*
8. *Jackson Browne*
9. *Bob Welch*
10. *Peter Brown*

Top Pop Female Artists

1. *Linda Ronstadt*
2. *Donna Summer*
3. *Dolly Parton*
4. *Olivia Newton-John*
5. *Yvonne Elliman*
6. *Natalie Cole*
7. *Debby Boone*
8. *Rita Coolidge*
9. *Roberta Flack*
10. *Crystal Gayle*

Top Pop Groups

1. *The Bee Gees*
2. *The Commodores*
3. *Fleetwood Mac*
4. *Foreigner*
5. *Styx*
6. *The Village People*
7. *Heatwave*
8. *K.C. & the Sunshine Band*
9. *Electric Light Orchestra*
10. *Kansas*

Best Pop Album Performers

1. *The Bee Gees*
2. *Fleetwood Mac*
3. *Linda Ronstadt*
4. *Barry Manilow*
5. *The Commodores*
6. *The Village People*
7. *Billy Joel*
8. *Chuck Mangione*
9. *Shaun Cassidy*
10. *Donna Summer*

Best Pop Singles Performers

1. *The Bee Gees*
2. *Andy Gibb*
3. *Billy Joel*
4. *Barry Manilow*
5. *Player*
6. *Linda Ronstadt*
7. *Debby Boone*
   Donna Summer TIE
8. *The Commodores*
9. *Steely Dan*
10. *Heatwave*

The 1979 Gallup Poll of Favorite Rock Entertainers

1. *Kiss*
2. *Boston*
3. *The Bee Gees*
4. *Foreigner*
5. *The Commodores*
6. *The Beatles*
7. *Led Zeppelin*
8. *Barry Manilow*
9. *Earth, Wind & Fire*
10. *Styx*
11. *Fleetwood Mac*
12. *The Rolling Stones*
13. *Aerosmith*
14. *Chicago*
15. *Meat Loaf*

Denver, David Bowie, the Osmonds, the Eagles, Joni Mitchell, Grand Funk Railroad, Lynyrd Skynyrd, Ted Nugent, and many others.

Today, Pop/Rock is an international institution — the renowned come from the United States, England, France, Australia, and various other countries, the stars tour every corner of the Earth, with the seemingly only exceptions of Antarctica, Greenland, upper Siberia, and a few remote jungle habitats. Anywhere that people will gather together to listen to contemporary music, Rock musicians will come to perform. The once little-known and often-frowned-upon form of music is now the primary subject of various publications like *Billboard, Rolling Stone,* and *Cash Box,* and it is regularly featured in such mass market magazines as *Playboy, Time, Newsweek, Esquire,* and others. Books now cover everything from encyclopedic presentations to biographies and reproductions of lyrics.

The 40 performers and groups honored here will not diminish in the Rock world. But because Rock is such an ever-changing, ever-challenging world and such an always fertile ground for new talents, they will have to at least make room for the new names that will eventually join them — candidates like Bob Welch, Debby Boone, Gerry Rafferty, Alicia Bridges, Bonnie Tyler, Nick Gilder, A Taste of Honey, Rick James, the Village People, Meat Loaf, Queen, the Cars, Heatwave, Chic, and whoever else may come along with the talent, inspiration, ambition, energy, devotion, and all the folds of fortune and chance that are needed for someone to make it to the top of today's Pop/Rock culture . . . and to stay there.

The Performers

Aerosmith

Scorecard

Platinum Albums — 3
Gold Albums — 6

Top Albums

*Aerosmith*** (1973)
*Get Your Wings** (1974)
*Toys in the Attic** (1975)
*Rocks** (1976)
*Draw the Line*** (1977)
*Live Bootleg*** (1978)

Memorable Singles

Same Old Song and Dance (1973)
Dream On (1973)
Train Kept A-Rollin (1974)
S. O. S. (1975)
Toys in the Attic (1975)
Sweet Emotion (1975)
Walk This Way (1975)
You See Me Crying (1975)
Last Child (1976)
Home Tonight (1976)
Back in the Saddle (1977)
Sight for Sore Eyes (1977)
Come Together (1978)

Current Recording Label:
Columbia Records

** Platinum Certification
 * Gold Certification

Steve Tyler — *Lead singer*
Joe Perry — *Lead guitarist*
Tom Hamilton — *Bass*

Brad Whitford — *Rhythm*
Joey Kramer — *Drums*

It was not always easy or lucrative for Aerosmith. "I can remember when we had our eviction notice in one hand and a management contract in the other," said Joe Perry, the group's lead guitarist. "We were really on the skids, trying to stay alive. We literally had no food or anything."

He was referring to the first year of Aerosmith's existence as a rock group back in 1970. Founded as a trio (Joe Perry, Steve Tyler, and Tom Hamilton), their first jobs were in a mountain resort area of New Hampshire. When that proved less than substantial, the group decided to try their luck in Boston, and added Brad Whitford and Joey Kramer to round out the band. The group managed bookings for a number of one-night stands and an occasional club date but nothing that could be called steady. In those days, they were also known to perform on the sidewalks outside Boston University for nothing more than the enjoyment of performing.

Those first few years were the trying ones — the one redeeming factor was the appreciation they received from those who heard their music, but there was very little money that came along with it. During that time, however, they turned themselves over to the talent management firm of Leber-Krebs Inc. in New York. The result was a carefully planned method of exposure in other areas of the country — city by city, area by area. Aerosmith moved out from Boston and it did not take long before they established themselves as one of the top hard-rock groups in the nation.

By early 1973, their first album, *Aerosmith,* was on the market, and it was a success. They took to the touring circuit in earnest then and played in most of the large auditoriums of the country, in practically all the major cities of the United States. Various singles were cut and other albums followed. By the mid-1970s, Aerosmith was being talked about as the "Biggest and best American hard-rock band in the world." By 1977, each one of their first four record albums had sold more than two million copies.

In 1978, Aerosmith toured and performed before the widest possible range of audiences. They had gone back to playing small clubs, performing for crowds perhaps no larger than a few hundred . . .for a basic purpose: to refresh themselves with the intimacy of them. At the same time, they headlined (along with Ted Nugent) at a California concert which set the world's record for attracting the largest crowd ever to pay to attend a music event — 207,000 people anteed up that March day to hear them perform live. They had come a long way from the skids Joe Perry remembered back in Boston.

The Bee Gees

Scorecard

Platinum Albums — 3
Platinum Singles — 2
Gold Albums — 6
Gold Singles — 9
Grammy Awards — 5

Top Albums

The Bee Gees First (1967)
Horizontal (1968)
Idea (1968)
Best of the Bee Gees* (1969)
Trafalger (1971)
2 Years On (1971)
To Whom It May Concern (1972)
Best of the Bee Gees, Vol. 2 (1973)
Mr. Natural (1974)
Main Course* (1975)
Children of the World** (1976)
Bee Gees Gold* (1976)
Saturday Night Fever** (1977)
Here At Last . . . The Bee Gees . . . Live**
  (1978)
Spirits Having Flown (1978)

Memorable Singles

Spicks and Specks (1967)
New York Mining Disaster 1941 (1967)
To Love Somebody (1967)
Holiday (1967)
Massachusetts (1967)
Words (1967)
I've Gotta Get a Message to You (1968)
I Started a Joke (1968)
Lonely Days* (1970)
How Can You Mend a Broken Heart*
  (1971)
Don't Want to Live Inside Myself (1971)
Alive (1972)
Saw a New Morning (1973)
Run to Me (1973)
Mr. Natural (1974)
Charade (1974)
Jive Talkin* (1975)
Nights on Broadway (1975)
Love So Right* (1975)
You Should Be Dancing* (1976)
Boogie Child (1976)
How Deep Is Your Love* (1977)
Stayin Alive** (1978)
Night Fever** (1978)
Too Much Heaven* (1978)
Tragedy (1979)

Grammy Awards

1977 Best Pop Vocal Performance,
     Group: *How Deep Is Your Love*
1978 Best Album of the Year: *Saturday
     Night Fever*
     Best Pop Vocal Performance:
     Saturday Night Fever
     Producers of the Year: *Saturday
     Night Fever*
     Best Arrangement for Voices:
     Stayin' Alive

Current Recording Label: RSO

** Platinum Certification
 * Gold Certification

Barry Gibb was nine years old, his younger brothers, the twins Robin and Maurice, only seven when they first took to the stage as a group in Manchester, England, back in 1956. Two years later, the family packed up and moved to Australia. There, the brothers Gibb were first signed to perform at a speedway stadium at Brisbane, presumably during times when the air was not filled with the roar of racing cars. But then, you have to start somewhere.

Still not yet teenagers, the Brothers Gibb adopted a new name to perform under: the Bee Gees. For the Bee Gees, however, fame was not all that swift in coming. It began gradually in Australia. After the short-lived gigs at the speedway, there was a fairly regular schedule of performances in person and on television through 1962. It was enough exposure to help make a mild success of their first single, *Three Kisses of Love,* released the following year.

During the next four years, the Bee Gees came out with a dozen more singles, but none of them left any noticeably indelible mark on the recording world. It was not until 1967 actually, when they issued the single *Spicks and Specks,* that their reputation as one of the top rock groups in Australia became well grounded. That was also the same year they left Australia to return to England. And it was also the year they made their debut on the American charts with another record, *New York Mining Disaster 1941.*

Through the 1960s, the Bee Gees' international reputation steadily grew, the nourishment coming from a continuing line of hit songs, television appearances, and a series of successful tours in Europe and the United States. But in 1969, internal trouble arose. First, Robin left the group to go it alone; a few months later Barry and Maurice decided to split up as well. The rift, however, lasted only until late 1970. They regrouped then and proceeded to produce a remarkable string of successful records.

Singles taken from *Saturday Night Fever* as well as other efforts in 1978 and 1979 staggered the record industry. Some statistics tell the story:

How Deep Is Your Love was in the "Top Ten" for 17 weeks, longer than any other single in the 20-year history of *Billboard* Magazine's "Hot 100." Three singles in succession reached No. 1 on the charts in 1978.
The Bee Gees had both the No. 1 and No. 2 records during the same week (no one since the Beatles back in 1964 had done that).
Barry Gibb wrote or co-wrote *nine* songs in 1978 that reached No. 1 on the charts.
At one point, the group had five singles in the "Top Ten" during the same week.

All that is not for lack of trying, either. The Bee Gees, since that first record back in 1963, have written more than 1000 songs.

Boston

Scorecard

Platinum Albums — 2
Gold Albums — 2

Top Albums

*Boston*** (1976)
*Don't Look Back*** (1978)

Memorable Singles

More Than a Feeling (1976)
Smokin' (1976)
Long Time (1977)
Let Me Take You Home Tonight (1977)
Peace of Mind (1977)
Foreplay (1977)
A Man I'll Never Be (1978)

Current Recording Label: Epic

** Platinum Certification

Tom Scholz — *Guitars, Keyboards*
Brad Delp — *Vocals*
Barry Goudreau — *Lead Guitar*

Fran Sheehan — *Bass*
Sib Hashian — *Drums*

A variety of businesses have been operated out of people's basements over the years, but Rock bands have rarely been found among them. Except Boston. Back in 1976, they began, for all practical purposes, in Tom Scholz's basement in Watertown, Massachusetts, and they are still recording from there today.

Today, however, Tom Scholz's basement has been turned into a first-class studio complex, equipped with a 24-track console replete with limiters, equalizers, function generators, compressors, and a spectrum analyzer. He has dubbed his subterranean workshop appropriately enough, Hideaway Studios.

The basement was only outfitted with a 12-track console when Scholz and his four colleagues and longtime friends Brad Delp, Barry Goudreau, Fran Sheehan, and Sib Hashian gathered there to record some of their songs. They produced a demo tape in Scholz's basement, however, that was so good musically and so proficient technically that Epic Records took it just as the group had produced it and turned it into an album — something absolutely unheard of in the regular mainstream of Rock music production.

Entitled simply *Boston*, the album was an instant hit, scaling the Charts in what was record time for a hitherto unknown group. The single spawned by it, *More Than a Feeling*, followed as another momentous winner. Within a few short weeks, incredible as it may seem, Boston went from a quintet experimenting in a basement studio to a national headline attraction in one of the most difficult businesses to crack, that of Pop/Rock music. "Our record had been out about three weeks," Barry Goudreau told a reporter, "and had gone gold before we played a gig."

Tom Scholz knew what he was doing, however, when he was puttering around his basement. He has a graduate degree from MIT (Massachusetts Institute of Technology) in mechanical engineering. And the group had been playing apart and together for several years before putting together that demo tape (they were reasonably popular in those earlier days, according to Scholz, at weddings, in various barrooms, and on Knights of Columbus hall stages in and around Boston).

Scholz and other members of Boston are perfectionists, both in terms of the music they play as well as in the way it is technically produced. Their second album, *Don't Look Back*, is a prime example of that. "We spent about 1000 hours in the studio," Scholz explained, "and about two years conceiving, playing, clipping, listening, and retaping . . . As many as eight or 10 guitars are used in some places where your ear will hear only one."

Scorecard

Platinum Albums — 2
Gold Albums — 5

Top Albums

Jackson Browne (1972)
*For Everyman** (1973)
*Late for the Sky** (1974)
*The Pretender*** (1976)
*Running on Empty*** (1977)

Memorable Singles

Doctor My Eyes (1972)
Rock Me on the Water (1972)
Redneck Friend (1973)
For Everyman (1973)
Late for the Sky (1974)
Ready or Not (1974)
Fountain of Sorrow (1975)
The Pretender (1976)
Here Come Those Tears (1977)

Current Recording Label: Asylum

** Platinum Certification
 * Gold Certification

Jackson Browne

In Greenwich Village back in 1967, Nico, chief vocalist of the sometimes kinky, sometimes dazzling group known as the Velvet Underground, was a top item at a club called the Electric Circus. Playing backup guitar for Nico was a 17-year-old performer/songwriter, working his first professional job. Jackson Browne was his name, and it did not take long at all for *his* talents to be appreciated.

Before Browne was 21, Nico had recorded several of the songs Browne had written. So had The Nitty Gritty Dirt Band, Linda Ronstadt, Johnny Rivers, and Steve Noonan, among others. As a performer, Jackson Browne made his first concert tour in 1970 and cut his first album, *Jackson Browne,* for release two years later. From that point on, his name became a standard in the industry.

When the name Jackson Browne first began to emerge in the select world of Pop/Rock music, it was attached to a young man who was looked on more as a poet of song than an entertainer. It was almost instantly clear that he was deeply talented songwriter, but he wanted both the self-satisfactions of creating music and performing it.

Jackson Browne may have debuted professionally in New York City but he came there by way of Heidelberg, Germany, where he was born in 1948 and Los Angeles where he had lived all but the first three years of his life. In high school in California, he took to writing his own songs and performing them in various local coffeehouses.

In 1972, with his reputation already established, he began his association with accompaniest David Lindley, and the arrangement has thrived ever since. That was also the year he went on his first professional tour, a journey through the United Kingdom with Joni Mitchell.

It was also the beginning of his personal recording career. The then-fledgling label who took the name Asylum added Jackson Browne to its roster of hopefuls. His first album made the Charts, and both he and Asylum have thrived ever since.

With Lindley as the nucleus, Jackson Browne formed his own touring band in 1973. Since then, they have toured nationally alone and with the likes of America, Linda Ronstadt, the Eagles, Bonnie Raitt and Phoebe Snow. All five of the albums he has recorded since 1972 have been certified gold by RIAA and the last two, *The Pretender* and *Running on Empty,* warranted the honor of platinum.

During the same period he has written songs that have been recorded by many of the most respectable names in the business: the Eagles, Joan Baez, Jackson 5, Joe Cocker, and others.

Among the very well-known titles he has penned for other performers are: *Take It Easy* and *James Dean* (for The Eagles) and *Jamaica Say You Will* (for Joe Cocker). His brother, Severin Browne, is also a recording artist.

The Captain & Tennille

Scorecard

Platinum Albums — 1
Gold Albums — 4
Gold Singles — 5
Grammy Awards — 1

Top Albums

*Love Will Keep Us Together** (1975)
Por Amour Viviremos (1976)
*Song of Joy*** (1976)
*Come in from the Rain** (1977)
*Greatest Hits** (1977)
Dream (1978)

Memorable Singles

*The Way I Want to Touch You** (1974)
*Love Will Keep Us Together** (1975)
Por Amor Viviremos (1975)
Sentirte (1975)
*Lonely Night** (1976)
Smile for Me One More Time (1976)
*Shop Around** (1976)
*Muskrat Love** (1976)
Can't Stop Dancing (1977)
Come in From the Rain (1977)
We Never Really Say Goodbye (1977)
Circles (1977)
You Need a Woman Tonight (1978)

Grammy Awards

1975 Record of the Year: *Love Will Keep Us Together*

Current Recording Label:
A & M Records

** Platinum Certification
 * Gold Certification

Daryl Dragon — his real name — is the Captain. Son of famous orchestra conductor Carmen Dragon, he studied classical piano for 10 years. Toni Tennille, product of Montgomery, Alabama and full partner in the duo, also spent nine of her youth years in classical piano training.

They met back in 1971 on the set of *Mother Earth*, a rock-ecology musical that Toni Tennille had co-written with a friend. (She was also the show's chief female vocalist.) *Mother Earth* was being presented at San Francisco's South Coast Repertory Theater when it suddenly found itself in need of a keyboardist. Daryl Dragon, between tours with the Beach Boys, was signed on.

He and Toni Tennille hit it off from the very beginning. Dragon arranged for Tennille to join the next tour of the Beach Boys, and she became the first and only female Beach Boy in the lengthy history of that illustrious group.

Because Daryl Dragon chose to wear a yachting captain's hat while performing during the tour, Mike Love of the Beach Boys coined the nickname Captain Keyboard for him. When he and Toni Tennille decided to strike out on their own, he formally adopted the name "the Captain," probably because it sounded better than The Dragon and Tennille.

They put the performing part of their act together in 1973 when Toni Tennille wrote a song for Daryl Dragon, *The Way I Want to Touch You.* It was to be their debut offering as a duo, but they could not convince a record company of the efficacy of producing it. So, they dug up $500 of their own money and brought the single out on a private label they called Butterscotch Castle Records.

While *The Way I Want to Touch You* was beginning to catch on in Los Angeles, The Captain and Tennille added the matrimonial part of their act, becoming a duo now in every sense of the word. Shortly after, A & M Records heard about the blossoming popularity of this new twosome and decided to sign them. The company was amply rewarded for its effort with the second single to come from Captain and Tennille. The song, from the pen of Neil Sedaka, was *Love Will Keep Us Together.* It won a Grammy award in 1975, and has since gone on to sell more than 2½ million copies. And, needless to say, it established The Captain & Tennille in today's Pop/Rock scene.

Five years earlier, Toni Tennille had been a file clerk in Los Angeles and Daryl Dragon was just surviving with a few small club dates and as a sometime touring member of the Beach Boys. Since that time, however, all their records have been charted in gold or platinum. They made their television debut in 1976, with a summer special. It was so well received that they were signed for their own variety show series for the following television season. As hosts of *The Captain & Tennille Show,* they proved to be as popular in the video medium as they had in the audio world of recording.

Chicago

Scorecard

Platinum Albums — 3
Gold Albums — 12
Gold Singles — 3

Top Albums

Chicago Transit Authority* (1969)
Chicago II* (1970)
Chicago III* (1971)
Chicago at Carnegie Hall* (1971)
Chicago V* (1972)
Chicago VI* (1973)
Chicago VII* (1974)
Chicago VIII* (1975)
Chicago IX* (1975)
Chicago X** (1976)
Chicago XI** (1977)
Hot Streets** (1978)

Memorable Singles

Questions (1969)
Colour My World (1970)
25 or 6 to 4 (1970)
*Does Anyone Really Know What
  Time It Is* (1970)
Free (1971)
Lowdown (1971)
Beginnings (1971)
Questions (1971)
I'm a Man (1971)
Saturday in the Park* (1972)
Now That You've Gone (1972)
Dialog (1972)
Feeling Stronger Every Day (1973)
Just You and Me* (1974)
Call on Me (1974)
Wishing You Were Here (1974)
Harry Truman (1975)
Old Days (1975)
Brand New Love Affair (1975)
Searchin' So Long (1975)
Another Rainy Day in New York City
  (1976)
If You Leave Me Now* (1976)
Together Again (1976)
Baby What a Big Surprise (1977)
Take Me Back to Chicago (1977)
Alive Again (1978)
No Tell Lover (1978)

Current Recording Label:
  Columbia Records

** Platinum Certification
 * Gold Certification

Peter Cetera — *Bass*
Robert Lamm — *Keyboards*
Walt Parazider — *Woodwinds*
Danny Seraphine — *Drums*
James Pankow — *Trombone*
Lee Loughnane — *Trumpet*
Laudir de Oliveira — *Percussion*
Donnie Dacus — *Guitar*

Only two members of today's Chicago were not there at the founding of this group back in the late 1960s. Laudir de Oliveira came aboard in 1974, and Donnie Dacus joined in 1978 after the death of guitarist Terry Kath. And of the original eight members, seven were residents of the city from which they took their name. The only renegade was Robert Lamm, who was born and raised in Brooklyn.

Chicago, which went under a variety of names in the early days, got off to a relatively slow start. The stages they took to in those early days were usually located in high school gymnasiums, American Legion halls, various small clubs and coffee houses, all of which were away from the primary entertainment roads in Chicago and its surrounding area. By 1969, they had adopted the name Chicago Transit Authority, apparently in honor of Chicago's metropolitan transportation system, and introduced their first album.

From the very beginning, Chicago was an innovative group. The members, most of them anyway, had had an impressive amount of formal music training and had developed into creative and original musicians. They managed to bring together a unique blend of Rock, rhythm & blues, and jazz. The outpouring of music that issued from them included both vocals and instrumentals, often varying considerably in length; and the uniqueness of their compositions and interpretations with their absorbing lyricism caught on just as soon as it was given proper exposure. Their first album moved onto the Charts, then worked its way up to gold certification. That's when they shortened their name.

By this time, however, Chicago was actually in residence in Los Angeles, their new base of operations. They were in the midst of planning their first set of tours, which would take them from LA back east across the United States, on to London, Tokyo, and an assortment of other international ports of call. Their second album, titled with their new name, *Chicago II,* continued — in fact furthered— the success they had achieved with the first. (It was *Cash Box* magazine's album of the year in 1970)

Chicago has been a prominent member of the Rock scene for 10 years now, and their popularity has not flagged once during that period, something that very few groups can claim. The group has maintained a steady flow of albums and singles that have all made the Charts, and they have continued to draw sell-out crowds to their live performances.

Eric Clapton

Scorecard

Platinum Albums — 2
Gold Albums — 11
Gold Singles — 3

Top Albums

(with Cream)

Fresh Cream* (1966)
Disraeli Gears* (1967)
Wheels of Fire* (1968)
Goodbye* (1969)
The Best of Cream* (1969)
Live Cream, Vol. 1 (1970)
Live Cream, Vol 2 (1972)
Heavy Cream (1973)

(with Blind Faith)

Blind Faith* (1969)

(with Derek and the Dominoes)

Layla and Other Assorted
  Love Songs* (1970)

(as a soloist)

Eric Clapton (1970)
History of Eric Clapton* (1972)
As His Best (1972)
Clapton (1973)
Rainbow Concert (1973)
461 Ocean Boulevard* (1974)
There's One in Every Crowd (1975)
E.C. Was Here (1975)
No Reason to Cry (1976)
Slowhand** (1977)
Backless** (1978)

Memorable Singles

(with Cream)

I Feel Free (1966)
Sunshine of Your Love* (1967)
Anyone for Tennis (1968)
White Room (1968)

(with Derek and the Dominoes)

Tell the Truth (1970)
Bell-Bottom Blues (1971)
Layla (1971)

(as a soloist)

After Midnight (1970)
Let It Rain (1972)
Bell Bottom Blues (1973)
I Shot the Sheriff* (1974)
Willie and the Hand Jive (1974)
Swing Low, Sweet Chariot (1975)
Knockin' on Heaven's Door (1975)
Carnival (1977)
Lay Down Sally* (1977)
Wonderful Tonight (1978)
Promises (1978)

Current Recording Label: RSO

** Platinum Certification
 * Gold Certification

He has been called "Guitar Hero of the World," the "Guitarist's Guitarist," and the "King of Rock Guitarists." And the people who have been referring to Eric Clapton in such rapturous terms have been doing it since the mid-1960s.

Since he took up the guitar at age 16 (late by most Rock star standards), Eric Clapton has moved about the contemporary music world with wanderlust. For more than 10 years, he would meander through a variety of groups before successfully launching and maintaining himself as a superstar solo, all the while commanding the utmost respect from his fellow entertainers.

In 1963, he was strumming rhythm & blues with a group called the Roosters in a smattering of London's small clubs of the day. As the year wore on, he switched to a better-known group, the Yardbirds. By 1965, he had moved on to John Mayall's Bluesbreakers, which proved to be a spawning ground for a number of today's top Rock musicians (the founding trio of Fleetwood Mac, for example).

A year later, however, Eric Clapton decided to form his own group with Bassist Jack Bruce and Drummer Ginger Baker, which became one of the most famous trios in Rock history — Cream — even though its life was very short. From its inception, Cream was an instant success in both America and Europe. Fans stormed the record stores for their albums and packed the auditoriums and stadiums where they performed live.

Cream lasted only until 1968, however, when the itinerant Eric Clapton departed for other musical adventures. He formed a new group called Blind Faith, but unlike Cream it was a failure. After that, it became a disheartening journey — less-than-spectacular stabs at soloing and various gigs with groups like Delaney and Bonnie and Derek and the Dominoes were not well received and Clapton's career was clearly on the downtrack. It had its effect on him. From mid-1970 to mid-1972, Eric Clapton, for all practical purposes, dropped out of the Rock world.

It was actually not until 1974 that Eric Clapton was lured back into the spotlight. This time it was as a true solo talent. The vehicle was the album 461 Ocean Boulevard, and it carried Clapton's career back to the top. The single from it, I Shot the Sheriff, virtually inundated the radio airwaves that year.

Solo records now flowed, so did re-releases and re-recordings of earlier Clapton works with various of his other groups. Eric Clapton's name has been on the Charts every year since that fateful comeback. Today, he is still the most respected guitarist in the business. And he has embellished that reputation with his vocalizations and song-writing. As one writer put it, "Clapton, long addicted to being a part of the group scene, is now a group himself."

The Commodores

Scorecard

Platinum Albums — 1
Gold Albums — 1

Top Albums

Machine Gun (1973)
Caught in the Act (1974)
Movin' On (1975)
Hot on the Tracks (1976)
Commodores (1977)
*Natural High*** (1978)
Greatest Hits (1978)

Memorable Singles

Machine Gun (1973)
Slippery When Wet (1974)
Sweet Love (1974)
Do the Bump (1975)
Just to Be Close to You (1975)
I Feel Sanctified (1976)
Fancy Dancer (1976)
This Is Your Life (1977)
Easy (1977)
Brick House (1978)
Too Hot to Trot (1978)

Current Recording Label: Motown

** Platinum Certification

Lionel Richie — *Lead Tenor, Saxophone*
Walter Clyde Orange — *Vocals, Drums*
Thomas McClary — *Guitarist*
Ronald LaPread — *Bass*
Milan Williams — *Keyboards*
William King — *Brass*

The Commodores introduced themselves on the Rock scene in late 1973 with their first album, *Machine Gun* — not locally as most groups do but on an international scale right from the beginning. The group's reception, in fact, was so overwhelming, with a following that grew so quickly and in such vast proportions, that they were quickly given the nickname the "Black Beatles."

The Commodores, however, are entirely a product of the Western Hemisphere, all of them born, bred, and still claiming residence in America's deep South. Their headquarters today is the small college town of Tuskegee, Alabama, which is also known as the town most associated with famous black educator Booker T. Washington.

Machine Gun was an immediate hit in the United States, and concurrently became a best-seller in Canada, the Far East, as well as various countries in Africa and Europe. To substantiate their sudden success, the Commodores took to the tour circuit shortly after the release of their first album. The United States was the first leg of the agenda, followed by Canada, then major cities in Europe, Japan, and the Philippine Islands. In the Philippines, as a matter of fact, they broke the all-time attendance record for a Rock concert which had been held for years by the Beatles.

The Commodores have followed *Machine Gun* with a best-selling album in each subsequent year. A spate of singles during the same six-year period has also kept their name on the *Billboard* "Hot 100" and their music on the radio airwaves of America. They continue to tour with great success — a recent European tour was completely sold out before the group even left the confines of the United States.

In 1978, the Commodores made their motion picture debut in the Motown/Casablanca production of *Thank God Its Friday*. In the movie, they starred with Donna Summer, who introduced her Grammy award winning song of that year, *Last Dance*. The Commodores contributed their hit single to the movie, *Too Hot to Trot*.

In early 1979, the famous Gallup Poll conducted an extensive survey to find out who were the most popular recording stars in the United States. Out of the hundreds of well-known Rock groups today, the Commodores were honored in the top five. Their company in that select group included the Bee Gees, Kiss, Foreigner, and Boston. Not bad for a little group from a small town in the South who decided only a few short years ago to make some music together.

Alice Cooper

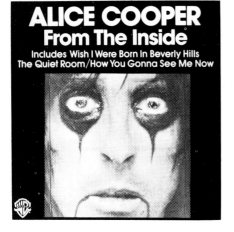

Scorecard

Gold Albums — 8
Gold Singles — 1

Top Albums

Pretties for You (1970)
Easy Action (1970)
Love It to Death* (1971)
School's Out* (1971)
Killer* (1971)
Billion Dollar Babies* (1973)
Muscle of Love* (1973)
Greatest Hits* (1974)
Welcome to My Nightmare* (1975)
Alice Cooper Goes to Hell* (1976)
Lace and Whiskey (1977)
The Alice Cooper Show (1977)
From the Inside (1978)

Memorable Singles

Return of the Spiders (1970)
I'm Eighteen (1971)
Caught in a Dream (1971)
Under My Wheels (1971)
Be My Lover (1972)
Raped and Freezin' (1973)
No More Mister Nice Guy (1973)
Billion Dollar Babies (1973)
Teen Age Lament '74 (1973)
Muscle of Love (1974)
Department of Youth (1975)
Only Women Bleed (1975)
Welcome to My Nightmare (1975)
I Never Cry* (1976)
Go to Hell (1976)
You and Me (1977)
It's Hot Tonight (1977)
How You Gonna See Me Now (1978)

Current Recording Label: Warner Bros.

* Gold Certification

Alice Cooper — the boy with the girl's name and the eerily painted face — is credited with introducing some of the most bizarre behavior before an audience in the history of live performance. Caressing writhing boa constrictors, tearing dolls limb from limb, throwing things into the audience, performing in a straight-jacket are just a few of Alice Cooper's quaint innovations on stage. Today, you can apply for membership in The Alice Cooper School for the Hopelessly Insane, and receive a certificate to show that you belong.

Alice Cooper was born Vincent Furnier in Detroit, Michigan, on February 4, 1948. Years later in Phoenix, Arizona, where his family had moved, he formed his first rock group along with four high school classmates. They called themselves the Earwigs. "We were upper middle class suburban brats," Cooper later referred to that first group. The Earwigs went through several name changes — the Spiders was one — and then uprooted itself in the late 1960s and moved to Los Angeles.

The first audience reactions to the outlandish performances of Alice Cooper and his colleagues were not too good. In some instances, astonished audiences simply walked out on the performance; on occasion they tried to storm the stage, apparently intending to do to Alice Cooper what he was doing to the baby dolls up there. People perhaps just weren't ready for Alice Cooper back in the late 1960s. The two albums they cut in those days were raucous and ear-shattering, and that was about all that was being said about them.

Word of weird goings-on with this strange act, however, began to spread — first in the rock underground and cult culture and then surfacing in the open (and commercial) world of Pop/Rock.

Alice Cooper's third album, *Love It to Death,* released in February 1971, changed the course of his career. It was a booming success, rising into *Billboard's* Top 20, and spawning a single, *I'm Eighteen.*

By 1973, Alice Cooper had a string of hit records and a notoriety all his own. Those who once watched in amazement or scratched their heads or questioned his sanity, now only did the latter. That year also signaled a split with the original group from Phoenix, and Alice Cooper hired some new faces to back him up.

In 1977, he took a brief vacation from the music world and checked into a hospital to dry out from a drinking problem. Not one to waste an experience, he used that sojourn as a springboard for his next album. *From the Inside* contains a variety of songs that explore the inner world of an insane asylum. He also requests all listeners to participate in his Alice Cooper Captive Audience & Choir and sing along with the grand finale to the record, a song consisting of only the words, "We're all crazy."

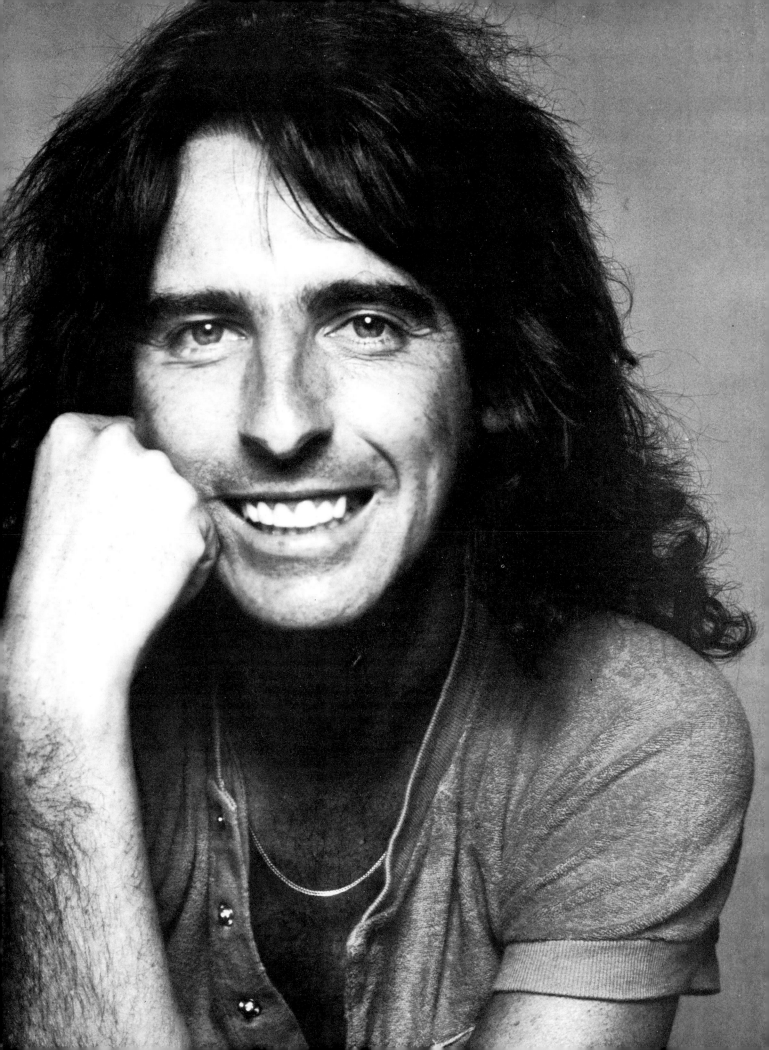

Neil Diamond

Scorecard

Platinum Albums — 4
Gold Albums — 13
Gold Singles — 5
Grammy Awards — 1

Top Albums

Just For You (1967)
Neil Diamond's Greatest Hits (1968)
Velvet Gloves and Spit (1968)
Touching You, Touching Me* (1969)
Gold* (1970)
Tap Root Manuscript* (1970)
Stones* (1971)
Moods* (1972)
Hot August Night* (1972)
Jonathan Livingston Seagull* (1973)
Greatest Hits* (1974)
Serenade* (1974)
And the Singer Sings His Song (1976)
Beautiful Noise** (1976)
Love at the Greek** (1977)
I'm Glad You're Here with Me Tonight**
  (1977)
You Don't Bring Me Flowers** (1978)

Memorable Singles

Solitary Man (1966)
Cherry, Cherry (1966)
I Got the Feelin (1966)
Girl You'll Be a Woman Soon (1967)
Kentucky Woman (1967)
Red Rubber Ball (1968)
Sweet Caroline* (1968)
Brother Love's Traveling Salvation Show
  (1969)
Holly Holy* (1969)
Touching You, Touching Me (1969)
Cracklin Rosie* (1970)
He Ain't Heavy, He's My Brother (1970)
Stones (1971)
Play Me (1972)
Song Sung Blue* (1972)
Walk on Water (1972)
Cherry, Cherry (1973)
Be (1973)
Skybird (1974)
I've Been This Way Before (1975)
The Last Picasso (1975)
If You Know What I Mean (1976)
Beautiful Noise (1976)
You Don't Bring Me Flowers Anymore*
  (1978)

Grammy Awards

1973 Best Original Score for a Motion
    Picture on TV: Jonathan Living-
    ston Seagull

Other Awards

1973 Oscar Best Original Score:
    Jonathan Livingston Seagull

Current Recording Label: Columbia
  Records

** Platinum Certification
 * Gold Certification

He was a pre-med student attending New York University on a scholarship for, suprisingly enough, the sport of fencing, He was Neil Diamond, and even then he was more interested in song-writing than he was in healing bodies or sword-fighting. It was the same Neil Diamond, in fact, who at 10 had taken to performing on the streets of Brooklyn with a few friends, calling themselves the Memphis Backstreet Boys.

In those college-age days, however, at the dawn of the 1960s, he hung around Greewich Village and spent much more of his time writing songs than he did studying. Six months before he was to graduate from NYU, he was offered a $50 a week job writing commercial songs. The call was too great, he took it and quit school.

Working out of a cubicle, he was assigned the task of turning out new music in bulk. It was an inglorious existence for anyone with Neil Diamond's talent. Finally, he just gave it all up, rented a loft on Broadway for $35 a month and set about writing the kind of music that he wanted to write. From there, it is all history.

His first single releases were on the label of Bang Records, a small independent producer that he quickly outgrew when his first three songs became almost immediate hits. He then signed with Uni Records which was later absorbed into MCA.

By the late 1960s, Neil Diamond was known as the young man who had written and performed such instant classics as Kentucky Woman; Girl, You'll Be a Woman Now; and Sweet Caroline.

It was, of course, just the beginning. The hit records flowed, one after the other, and so did the critical acclaim. His one-man shows in the United States and abroad were among the most spectacular successes in the rock business. All the while, he continued to write music. Some of it he performed himself, other songs were written for the biggest names in the business — Frank Sinatra and Elvis Presley, among them.

By 1972, he had the stardom and the money that goes with it in the rock world. He went off the tour circuit then so he could devote more time to his musical writing. It would be a four-year respite from that aspect of the rock show world, one which many feel is the most grueling and draining for any performer. During that time, he continued his normal songwriting and also produced the original score album for the motion picture Jonathan Livingston Seagull.

In 1976, however, he took to the road again, first in Australia and New Zealand, then a whirlwind tour of the United States where he played to SRO house after SRO house. It was clear he had not lost touch with his audiences.

The new song hits continued right along, too, culminating perhaps in late 1978 when he teamed with Barbra Streisand to perform a song he had written: You Don't Bring Me Flowers Anymore. It was a multi-million seller, and one that prompted a writer to observe: "They are to the vocal what Fred Astaire and Ginger Rogers were to the dance."

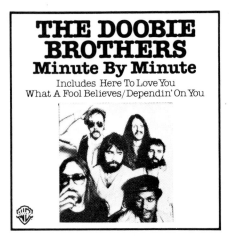

Doobie Brothers

Jeff Baxter — *Vocals, Guitar*
John Hartman — *Percussion*
Patrick Simmons — *Guitar*

Keith Knudsen — *Percussion*
Tiran Porter — *Bass*
Michael McDonald — *Keyboards*

Scorecard

Platinum Albums — 2
Gold Albums — 8
Gold Singles — 1

Top Albums

The Doobie Brothers (1971)
*Toulouse Street** (1972)
*The Captain and Me** (1973)
*What Were Once Vices** (1974)
*Stampede** (1975)
*Takin' It to the Streets*** (1976)
*The Best of the Doobie Brothers*** (1976)
*Livin' on the Fault Line** (1977)
*Minute by Minute** (1978)

Memorable Singles

Nobody (1971)
Listen to the Music (1972)
Toulouse Street (1972)
Jesus Is Just Alright (1972)
Long Train Runnin' (1973)
Evil Woman (1973)
*Black Water** (1974)
You Just Can't Stop It (1974)
Nobody (1974)
Take Me in Your Arms (1975)
Sweet Maxine (1975)
I Cheat the Hangman (1975)
Music Man (1975)
Takin' It to the Streets (1976)
Wheels of Fortune (1976)
Little Darling (1977)
Dependin' on You (1978)

Current Recording Label: Warner Bros.

** Platinum Certification
 * Gold Certification

The present-day, six-man Doobie Brothers band — none of whom have ever been related by blood — proliferated in the years since its birth back in 1970. The group began as a trio with the name Pud, grew to seven members at one time, and then shrunk back to six in 1977.

Only John Hartman of the original threesome is still with the Doobie Brothers today. Tom Johnston and Greg Murphy, the other founding members, have gone their own ways. Those three young men, however, were the ones who introduced the group out in San Jose in an assortment of small clubs in that city and in the area which surrounded it in northern California.

Patrick Simmons joined the group before that inaugural year ended and the new four-man Doobie Brothers, armed with demo tapes, convinced Warner Bros. Records to offer them a recording contract. Their first album on that label, *The Doobie Brothers,* was released in the spring of 1971. It was received with apathy.

By late 1971, Greg Murphy had left the group and so had his short-term replacement Dave Shogren. Tiran Porter was enlisted to fill the vacant bass guitarist slot. A fifth member, drummer Michael Hossack, was also signed on.

The Doobie Brothers were resilient, however. In early 1972, they came out with another album, *Toulouse Street* and a single, *Listen to the Music,* and this time neither of the recordings were received with indifference, both climbed to the top of the Charts.

In 1973, Michael Hossack resigned and Keith Knudsen, who had drummed with Lou Michaels, took his place. The next year, guitarist and vocalist Jeff Baxter left Steely Dan to take up residence with the Doobie Brothers. Michael McDonald, another renegade from Steely Dan, joined the following year, enlarging the group to a septet. Then the Doobie Brothers dropped back to a six-man band when Tom Johnston decided to crack out as a solo in 1977.

Their success as a performing and recording group has been a sustained fact since they cut their second album back in '72. A prime reason, of course, is the quality of the music they turn out, which *Billboard* magazine referred to as "a fusion of jazz, soul, and rock [which] continues to become more intricate and arresting."

Television is a medium that the Doobie Brothers of the late 1970s also conquered with a variety of guest appearances and specials. They can also claim the fact that they are probably the only Rock group around that boasts of having sponsored a celebrity golf classic — a benefit for the United Way.

Earth, Wind & Fire

Scorecard

Platinum Albums — 3
Gold Albums — 7
Gold Singles — 4
Grammy Awards — 4

Top Albums

Earth, Wind and Fire (1971)
Need of Love (1971)
Last Days and Time (1972)
*Head to the Sky** (1973)
*Open Our Eyes** (1974)
Another Time (1974)
*That's The Way of the World** (1975)
*Gratitude** (1975)
*Spirit*** (1976)
*All 'N All*** (1977)
The Best of Earth, Wind & Fire, Vol. 1
   (1977)

Memorable Singles

Fan the Fire (1971)
Where Have All the Flowers Gone (1973)
Evil (1973)
Keep Your Head to the Sky (1973)
Mighty, Mighty (1974)
Kalimba Story (1974)
Devotion (1974)
Hot Dawgit (1974)
*Shining Star** (1975)
Sun Goddess (1975)
That's the Way of the World (1975)
Reasons (1975)
Can't Hide Love (1975)
*Singasong** (1975)
Saturday Nite (1976)
*Getaway** (1976)
Departure (1976)
Serpentine Fire (1977)
Fantasy (1977)
Runnin' (1978)
Got to Get You into My Life (1978)
September (1978)

Grammy Awards

1975 Best Rhythm & Blues Performance
      Group: *Shining Star*
1978 Best Rhythm & Blues Performance
      Group: *All 'N All*
      Best Rhythm & Blues Instrumental:
      Runnin'
      Best Arrangement Accompanying
      Vocalists: *Gotta Get You into
      My Life*

Current Recording Label: Columbia
   Records

** Platinum Certification
* Gold Certification

Maurice White — *Vocals, Drums, Kalimba*
Verdine White — *Vocals, Bass, Percussion*
Philip Bailey — *Vocals, Percussion*
Larry Dunn — *Keyboards, Synthesizer*
Al McKay — *Guitars, Percussion*
Johnny Graham—*Guitars*
Andrew Woolfolk — *Saxophones, Flute*
Fred White — *Percussion*
Ralph Johnson — *Vocals, Percussion*

The scene is an intensely visual one. On stage, the singers and musicians are in constant motion, a piano player and his instrument are suspended and revolving in the air above, plumes of smoke belch upward from the stage floor. The music is a strange but captivating blend of Rock, soul, and jazz.

As the group's founder and present-day leader, Maurice White, puts it: "We are a free entity in life, and that's the way our music comes about. I would never put myself in a bag where I would have boundaries that would not permit me to experiment and explore."

In the 1960s, Maurice White moved from a black ghetto in Chicago to the Chicago Conservatory of Music to a place in the touring band of jazzman Ramsey Lewis. By 1969, the urge to branch out on his own had become too compelling and so, with his brother Verdine, he put together a band and named it for the most basic of natural elements — the earth, the wind, and fire.

During the next 10 years, the people who made up Earth, Wind & Fire would change periodically. In fact, the only two members of the original group remaining today are Maurice and Verdine White. The other current members came during the 1973-75 period. And the last to join was also the youngest of the musically-oriented White brothers, Fred. He signed on in 1975.

Earth, Wind & Fire, it could be said, endured the first few years of its existence. Three record albums were produced in 1971 and 1972, but neither did much to make the group known on a national level. *Head to the Sky*, the album released in 1973, however, changed all that. Three new members had joined the group for this album (Al McKay, Johnny Graham, and Andrew Woolfolk). The album made it to the top of the Charts and eventually earned gold certification.

Following that was a string of singles and albums that dotted the charts each year and rung up an impressive array of awards for quality, including everything from the Grammy to various American Music Awards.

Their motion picture debut was the movie soundtrack for *That's the Way of the World*, which as an album went on to earn an RIAA gold certification. Their next venture in the motion picture medium was an appearance in the 1978 movie *Sgt. Pepper's Lonely Hearts Club Band*, and their rendition of the Beatles' classic *Gotta Get You into My Life* was the only cut from the ensuing album that became a gold-record single.

Emerson, Lake & Palmer

Scorecard

Gold Albums 8

Top Albums

Emerson, Lake & Palmer* (1971)
Tarkus* (1971)
Pictures at an Exhibition* (1972)
Trilogy* (1972)
Brain Salad Surgery* (1973)
Welcome Back, My Friends . . .* (1974)
Works, Vol. I* (1976)
Works, Vol. II* (1977)
Love Beach (1978)

Memorable Singles

Lucky Man (1971)
Nutrocker (1972)
From the Beginning (1972)
I Believe in Father Christmas (1975)
Humbug (1975)
Fanfare for the Common Man (1977)
Brain Salad Surgery (1977)

Current Recording Label: Atlantic

* Gold Certification

Keith Emerson — *Keyboards*
Greg Lake — *Vocals, Guitar, Bass*
Carl Palmer — *Drums*

ELP, as they often refer to themselves, came to life in 1970. Keyboardist Keith Emerson was touring the United States that year with a British group called Nice when he met Greg Lake, the vocalist and bass guitarist with another group from England, King Crimson, who also happened to be touring the States that year.

Neither group was maintaining the stature and integrity, the two musicians felt, that was equivalent to their goals. They talked about breaking away, creating their own group, and fashioning its output to their own exacting standards. What they needed, they agreed, was a top-flight percussionist who shared their concept of the group. Finally, they happened on Carl Palmer who was performing with Atomic Rooster, a group he had established himself. They persuaded him to join up — and Emerson, Lake & Palmer was officially born.

The trio wanted to combine the strong appreciation of classical music all three held with their love for rock. As Keith Emerson later described it: "If you're looking for a description of what ELP is about, it's progressive rock with a lot of regard for the past."

After a trial run in Plymouth, an English seaside town, they formally opened at a major British rock festival on the Isle of Wight in 1970. The firing of a pair of cannons signaled their introduction. It was appropriate because ELP was an explosive success from that moment on. Their first album, simply titled *Emerson, Lake & Palmer*, released in 1971, soared to the top of the Charts both in England and the United States. Their tour dates in both countries were instant sell-outs.

ELP, from its very inception, experimented with new innovations. Keith Emerson was a pioneer back in 1972 with his use of the Moog Synthesizer. Shortly after that, Carl Palmer introduced the use of synthesized percussion to the rock world.

Although the group is as serious as any about the music they create, their live appearances have been far from subdued. On stage, they have wreaked a variety of violence on their instruments, leaped, contorted, knelt, and gyrated madly as they performed. The wildest unquestionably is Keith Emerson. "A concert is all-around entertainment," he said. "You have to exaggerate some points theatrically to express what you're doing musically."

The group, for all practical purposes, took a two-year vacation during 1975-76. They followed it with a spectacular comeback in the form of the starkly original and deeply moving album *Works*.

The music of Emerson, Lake & Palmer today ranks among the highest in serious critical appraisals — the product of innovators and unique stylists who have managed to package the highest standards of rock music with the least of inhibitions in performance.

Fleetwood Mac

FLEETWOOD MAC
Rumours
Includes the Hit Go Your Own Way
Also Includes Dreams
The Chain/Don't Stop/Songbird

Mick Fleetwood — *Drums*
John McVie — *Bass*
Christine McVie — *Vocals, Keyboards*

Lindsey Buckingham — *Vocals, Guitar*
Stevie Nicks — *Vocals*

In the more than 10 years that Fleetwood Mac has claimed that name, the group has been kaleidoscopic, the faces changing regularly with seemingly nothing more than the flick of a wrist. As a unit, the present Fleetwood Mac has only been together since 1975.

Two faces have been there from the very beginning — Mick Fleetwood and John McVie. Back in 1967, along with guitarist Peter Green, they founded the group after breaking away from John Mayall's Bluesbreakers, one of England's most popular blues bands of the day.

Green and Fleetwood actually started out together before that with a short-lived group called Shotgun Express that also featured the talents of a then-novice singer named Rod Stewart. To flesh out the original Fleetwood Mac, Jeremy Spencer (vocals and guitar) and Danny Kirwan (a guitarist) were enlisted.

In 1970, Peter Green left and John McVie's wife Christine came over from a group called Chickenshack. Then Jeremy Spencer, on tour with the group in Los Angeles, shaved his head, joined a religious cult called Children of God, and renounced rock music forever. Vocalist and guitarist Bob Welch than added his presence to Fleetwood Mac. In 1972, Danny Kirwan left and vocalist Dave Walker and guitarist Bob Weston signed on. A year later, both of them were gone, and in 1974, Bob Welch departed to form his own group (which he called Paris). In 1975, Stevie Nicks and Lindsey Buckingham joined up.

Fleetwood Mac had been popular in England almost from its very inception back in 1967. Over the next eight years, the group received some recognition in the United States, mostly on FM radio in the beginning then later as a result of several national tours. It was not until 1975, however, that Fleetwood Mac truly established itself at the very top of American rock music. That year, they introduced the album *Fleetwood Mac*, which became their first gold and subsequently platinum album. The album has since sold more than 3½ million copies, and three national hit singles were drawn from it *(Over My Head, Rhiannon,* and *Say You Love Me).*

Today, Fleetwood Mac is at the peak of its popularity, both on the concert stage as well as on records and tapes. Through all the changes of faces and bodies, the group has developed, matured, and kept an amazing stability as members came and went. As to where they are going from here, Lindsey Buckingham probably said it best: "We can't really say where we're going because idea-wise we're always a little ahead of ourselves, which is the best creative situation a band can be in."

Scorecard

Platinum Albums—1
Gold Albums—4
Gold Singles—1
Grammy Awards—1

Top Albums

Fleetwood Mac* (1968)
English Rose (1969)
Play On (1969)
Kiln House (1970)
Future Games (1971)
Bare Trees* (1972)
Penguin (1973)
Mystery to Me* (1973)
Heroes Are Hard to Find (1974)
Fleetwood Mac (1975)
Rumours** (1977)
The Original Fleetwood Mac (1977)

Memorable Singles

Black Magic Woman (1968)
Need Your Love So Bad (1968)
Oh Well (1969)
Sands of Time (1971)
Jewel-Eyed Judy (1971)
The Green Manlishi (1972)
Sentimental Lady (1972)
Remember Me (1973)
Did You Ever Love Me (1973)
For Your Love (1973)
Heroes Are Hard to Find (1974)
Over My Head (1975)
Rhiannon (1976)
Say You Love Me (1976)
Go Your Own Way (1976)
Dreams (1977)
Don't Stop (1977)
You Make Lovin' Fun (1977)

Grammy Awards

1977 Album of the Year: *Rumours*

Current Recording Label: Warner Bros.

** Platinum Certification
* Gold Certification

Foreigner

Mick Jones — *Lead Guitar, Vocals*
Ian McDonald — *Guitars, Keyboards, Horns, Vocals*
Lou Gramm — *Lead Vocals*

Al Greenwood — *Keyboards, Synthesizer*
Ed Gagliardi — *Bass, Vocals*
Dennis Elliott — *Drums*

Scorecard

Platinum Albums — 2
Gold Albums — 2
Gold Singles — 2

Top Albums

Foreigner** (1977)
Double Vision** (1978)

Memorable Singles

Feels Like the First Time (1977)
Woman, Oh Woman (1977)
Cold As Ice (1977)
Long, Long Way from Home (1977)
Double Vision* (1978)
Blue Morning, Blue Day (1978)
Hot Blooded* (1978)

Current Recording Label: Atlantic

** Platinum Certification
 * Gold Certification

Foreigner is one of the newest star clusters in the Pop/Rock sky, making what turned out to be a startling debut in the early months of 1977. The seed of the idea that was to become Foreigner, however, was planted a year earlier with two expatriate Englishmen, Mick Jones and Ian McDonald, who were living and working in New York City at the time.

For a long time Mick Jones had been harboring the thought of forming his own group. He had come to America as part of the British group Spooky Tooth, but by 1976 that group had dissolved. With its demise he stayed on in the USA, making it as a songwriter and session player. Ian McDonald, on the other hand, was an alumnus of both King Crimson and his own group McDonald and Giles. Both of those groups had gone the way of Spooky Tooth. McDonald, too, stayed on in New York, paying his way by working sessions and occasionally producing records. The time was right for both of them in 1976. Jones made the initial approach. As McDonald put it: "He asked me if I was doing anything for the next five years."

The two young men then started a search for a compatible group of musicians to round out the group. The first acquisition was keyboardist Al Greenwood, a native New Yorker who was performing then with a band called Storm. Next was Lou Gramm whose vocals with the group Black Sheep had impressed Mick Jones earlier.

Drummer Dennis Elliott was imported from England after an itinerant career there with various groups. Ed Gagliardi, another New York area inhabitant, added his bass guitar and vocalizations to complete the group.

The group's first effort was the album *Foreigner*. With its release and a whirlwind tour of the United States by the group, Foreigner became an overnight sensation. That first album alone has already passed the three million mark in number of copies sold. Their first tour was an equally dazzling success. The houses they played to were consistently SRO; they even became the first Rock act whose debut at Los Angeles' famous Greek Theatre was a total sell-out.

Following the U.S. circuit tour, the group went abroad to experience equally ecstatic receptions in such far-flung places as Hong Kong, Japan, Australia, continental Europe, and England.

For 1977, Foreigner was nominated for the Grammy Award as Best New Artist of the Year. Today, live and on records, there is no group hotter than Foreigner. But they're just as serious today about the music they produce as they were when they were forming the group. As Mick Jones told a reporter from *Rolling Stone:* "We're far more interested in trying to make good music that will send shivers down our spines than in trying to be the perfect Rock group."

Scorecard

Platinum Albums — 2
Gold Albums — 3

Top Albums
  (with Humble Pie)

As Safe as Yesterday Is (1969)
Town and Country (1969)
Humble Pie (1970)
Rock On (1971)

  (as soloist)

Wind of Change (1972)
Frampton's Camel (1973)
Something's Happened (1974)
Frampton* (1975)
Frampton Comes Alive** (1976)
I'm in You** (1977)

Memorable Singles

Jumping Jack Flash (1972)
Somethin's Happening (1974)
Show Me the Way (1975)
Baby, I Love Your Way (1975)
I'll Give You Money (1975)
Show Me the Way (1976)
Baby, I Love Your Way (re-release)
  (1976)
Do You Feel Like We Do (1976)
I'm in You (1977)
Signed, Sealed, Delivered (1977)

Current Recording Label:
  A & M Records

** Platinum Certification
 * Gold Certification

Peter Frampton

A brief 14 years after he was born in Bromley, one of the 32 boroughs of Greater London, Peter Frampton was performing in public. A guitarist and vocalist in those early days, as he still is today, Frampton was quick to come to the attention of England's teeny-boppers of the mid-1960s.

At the young age of 16, Peter Frampton was a solidly installed member of the popular British band called Herd. The following year, along with friend Steve Marriot, he formed another group and named it Humble Pie. The result of his collaboration with Marriot was four albums and a substantial following of fans in England. His affiliation with Humble Pie began to wind down at the start of the 70s. Frampton then made himself available as a studio guitarist to back up such superstars of the day as George Harrison (Beatles), John Entwistle (The Who), and soloist Harry Nilsson.

At age 21, he decided to leave the group scene altogether. The following year, he introduced his first solo album *Wind of Change*. It was less than a success, but he was still looked on by A & M Records as one of the really promising young rock musicians of the day.

The success he knows today did not, however, come that fast. His early records were critically well-received, but there was only a meager response at the record counters. In fact, it took Peter Frampton almost 4 years before he became the mega-star he is today. The catalyst in that transformation appeared in January 1976; it was the release of his fourth album, *Frampton Comes Alive*, which ironically enough, was almost an afterthought. Before agreeing to record it and harried because of the lack of success up to that point in his career, Frampton was seriously entertaining the idea of chucking the solo route and going back to the much simpler life of a session musician.

Frampton Comes Alive, however, literally assaulted the American Rock scene, and quickly marched to the top of the Charts. He followed it with a string of eminently successful singles, and the name Peter Frampton was suddenly a Rock standard in both the United States and Europe. He obviously gave up all thoughts of turning to the non-entity of a session musician. His popularity was so overwhelming, it prompted one rock encyclopedist to begin his biographical entry with: "Peter Frampton is the biggest superstar to emerge during the seventies."

Despite the astonishing success he had suddenly encountered and the worldwide recognition that came almost overnight, Frampton remained relatively untouched by it all. He is still looked upon as one of Rock music's most unaffected individuals. His answer when he was asked about his new-found stardom is perhaps the key to the Frampton personality: "I'm still knocked out at the fact that all the attention, the success and so forth, came when it did. I was blessed enough to be prepared for it."

Aretha Franklin

At age 14, Aretha Franklin was a gospel singer, impressing the congregations at the New Bethel Baptist Church in Detroit with the amazing range of her vocal talents. Four years later, she channeled those assets into the professional world of Soul and Rhythm & Blues. And today she is rightfully known as the world's First Lady of Soul.

She was 18 years old when she left Detroit for New York City and a crack at a career in the music business. It was at the urging of Major "Mule" Holly, a bass player for jazz pianist Teddy Wilson, who was among the first to sense the breadth of Aretha Franklin's talent. Shortly after her arrival in Manhattan, she was signed by John Hammond of Columbia Records (who had also recruited for that label such stars as Count Basie, Billie Holiday, and Bob Dylan).

For Aretha Franklin, the years in the early 1960s were not especially successful. Granted, some of her recordings during those years made the Charts, but they did not really climb very high on them. Nor was her name quite the household word it would later become. Personal appearances in those days were pretty much limited to small clubs in and around New York or as an opener or tag-along at concerts that featured bigger Rock names of the day.

1967, however, was the year that 25-year-old Aretha Franklin turned it all around. Just before the year began, she signed with Atlantic Records. They sent her to the now classic Soul music studios in Muscle Shoals, Alabama, for her first record on their label. It was the single *I Never Loved a Man (The Way I Love You),* which shortly after its release rose all the way to the No. 1 spot on the Charts. Her first Atlantic album followed the month after, and it became a best-seller too.

When the year 1967 ended, Aretha Franklin was the most sensational new star on the Rock and Rhythm & Blues scene. She was awarded two Grammies for her work that year, captured other awards from *Billboard, Cash Box,* and *Record World,* and half-way through the following year made the cover of *Time* magazine. Her Grammy awards were the first she would win in what would turn out to be an unprecedented string of eight straight years in which she would capture a Grammy.

Her tours took Aretha center-stage to the largest concert halls and stadiums in America as well as the major cities in Europe. And she was instantly one of the most sought-after guests on television.

Over the next 12 years, Aretha Franklin's recording output would be prodigious. Sales of her singles and albums would be tabulated in the multi, multi millions; the profusion of awards for the quality of her work would be unequalled in the world of Rhythm & Blues. Today, she records and tours as vigorously as ever and also devotes a large amount of her time to charity and benefit performances.

Andy Gibb

Scorecard

Platinum Albums — 2
Platinum Singles — 1
Gold Albums — 2
Gold Singles — 4

Top Albums

Flowing Rivers** (1977)
Shadow Dancing** (1978)

Memorable Singles

Words and Music (1976)
I Just Want to Be Your Everything*
(1977)
(Love Is) Thicker than Water* (1977)
Shadow Dancing** (1978)
Our Love, Don't Throw It All Away
(1978)
An Everlasting Love* (1978)

Current Recording Label: RSO

** Platinum Certification
 * Gold Certification

There is a little bar that caters to tourists on Ibiza, a resort-filled island in the Mediterranean just off the east coast of Spain. Back in the summer of 1970, a 13-year-old youngster of English citizenry, who had, however, grown up in Australia, used to perform there for vacationing crowds.

He would sing, accompanying himself on the guitar, and everyone who heard him thought he had remarkable talents. His name — Andy Gibb — was not at all familiar to the tourists from Europe and America who inhabited that bar. Most of them did not know either that his three older brothers — Barry, Robin, and Maurice — were also rock musicians who at that time were very real international celebrities performing under the name of the Bee Gees.

Andy Gibb was born 11 years after his oldest brother Barry, nine years after the twins, Robin and Maurice. The birthplace was Manchester, England, but Andy lived there for only six months before the family moved to Australia.

By the time Andy Gibb was nine years old, the Bee Gees were already a substantial success and the family had moved back to England. By the time he became a teenager, Andy decided he too would like to have a try at the same kind of career as his brothers.

In 1973, Andy, at 16, lined up his first group, composed of some local musicians of Britain's Isle of Man where the itinerant Gibb family was then living. After that, apparently taking cue from the success story of his brothers, he decided to go back to Australia to serve his apprenticeship there, where the Bee Gees had some 10 years earlier. It took Andy only a year there, however, to firmly establish his reputation. He did it with a series of regular concert performances and his first single record *Words and Music,* which he wrote himself. It was a success, at least in Australia.

After that, he made his way to the United States to meet up with his brothers, who were working in Miami, Florida, at the time. The four Gibb brothers collaborated on writing several songs there. Some of these would turn up on Andy Gibb's first album, *Flowing Rivers,* which was released in the summer of 1977. He continued on in the United States — live performances as well as TV where he appeared on everything from American Bandstand to an Olivia Newton-John special. A solo North American concert tour followed and it was smashingly successful.

A string of Top of the Chart singles and his second album, *Shadow Dancing,* brought him to the top of the rock business in 1978. He was nominated for two Grammy awards that year: Best New Artist of the Year and Best Pop Vocal Performance, Male.

Today, he composes his own songs but also writes others with older brother Barry.

Billy Joel

Scorecard

Platinum Albums — 2
Gold Albums — 3
Gold Singles — 1
Grammy Awards — 2

Top Albums

Cold Spring Harbor (1972)
Piano Man* (1973)
Streetlife Serenade (1974)
Turnstiles (1976)
The Stranger** (1977)
52nd Street** (1978)

Memorable Singles

Captain Jack (1972)
Piano Man (1973)
The Entertainer (1974)
Movin' Out (1977)
Just the Way You Are* (1977)
My Life (1978)

Grammy Awards

1978 Best Song of the Year: Just the
    Way You Are
    Best Record of the Year: Just the
    Way You Are

Current Recording Label: Columbia
Records

** Platinum Certification
 * Gold Certification

On a February evening in 1979, emcee of the night John Denver announced from the stage of the Shrine Auditorium in Los Angeles that the Grammy for Best Record of 1978 was awarded to Billy Joel for a song he both wrote and performed, Just the Way You Are. It was one of two Grammies Joel won that evening, just about the highest honor a rock recording artist can earn.

A top singer-songwriter of the 70s, Billy Joel is the same young man once known as William Martin who took classical piano lessons when he was four years old all the way until he stowed that 12 years later and joined his first rock band.

Billy Joel likes to think of himself as a product of the city streets, and the songs he has written often reflect that background. At 16, he dropped out of high school to devote full time to his music and formed a group called the Echoes.

During the next four years, the Echoes became the Lost Souls, then the Emerald Lords, and finally nothing at all. Billy Joel then joined with another group called the Hassles whose performances too were pretty much restricted to the local Long Island area.

Performing was not synonymous with earning a living for Billy Joel in those days. To pay the bills he worked from time to time in a factory and at other assorted jobs. He even recorded a commercial with Chubby Checker for Bachman Pretzels.

In 1972, the first real break came. He cut a full album of songs he had written. It was called Cold Spring Harbor. Joel and the group who recorded the LP with him toured the country to promote it. The days of regionalism had ended.

After the release of Cold Spring Harbor and the promotional tour, Billy Joel moved to California. The band, however, broke up when they found they were not making an adequate living off their efforts as a group. To keep some food on his own table during those times, Joel fell back on his piano-playing abilities and worked various piano bars under his real name of Bill Martin. He capitalized on this otherwise unhappy way of performing by writing the song Piano Man, which became the title song for his new album. The album changed everything. It was a smash success, and Billy Joel's days of playing the piano in cabarets were over forever.

By 1975, he was back in New York, but this time he was performing in places like Carnegie Hall and the Lincoln Center, and not dingy clubs or high school gymnasiums out on Long Island. He revamped his band and began turning out a fresh series of songs. His name soared to the top of the rock industry. With it came the awards, the financial success, the critical acclaim for his efforts. But none of that, it seems, really ever got to him. "You just go with the moment," he said. "I'll always be a musician. Since I was four years old I've been a musician. And I don't want to stop doing that. I like it too much."

Scorecard

Platinum Albums — 3
Gold Albums — 15
Gold Singles — 10

Top Albums

Elton John* (1970)
Tumbleweed Connection* (1971)
Madman Across the Water* (1971)
Friends (soundtrack)* (1971)
Honky Chateau* (1972)
Don't Shoot Me, I'm the Only Piano
 Player* (1973)
Goodbye Yellow Brick Road* (1973)
Caribou* (1974)
Greatest Hits* (1974)
Empty Sky (1975)
Captain Fantastic and the Brown Dirt
 Cowboy* (1975)
Rock of the Westies* (1975)
Here and There* (1976)
Blue Moves** (1976)
Greatest Hits, Vol.2** (1977)
A Single Man** (1978)

Memorable Singles

Lady Samantha (1970)
Border Song (1970)
Friends (1971)
Levon (1971)
Tiny Dancer (1972)
Rocket Man (1972)
Honky Cat (1972)
Crocodile Rock* (1972)
Daniel (1973)
Goodbye Yellow Brick Road* (1973)
Bennie and the Jets* (1974)
Don't Let the Sun Go Down on Me*
 (1974)
The Bitch Is Back (1974)
Lucy in the Sky with Diamonds* (1974)
Philadelphia Freedom* (1975)
Someone Saved My Life Tonight* (1975)
Island Girl* (1975)
Grow Some Funk of Your Own (1976)
Don't Go Breaking My Heart* (1976)
Sorry Seems to Be the Hardest Word*
 (1976)
Shoulder Holster (1976)
Part Time Love (1978)

Current Recording Label: MCA Records

** Platinum Certification
 * Gold Certification

Elton John

Elton John has spent more money buying wildly ornate eyeglasses than most people have in purchasing a house. But then Elton John has earned more money performing than the collective income of a small city-full of people. It is all part of the Elton John image — which is in turn so much a part of Rock history.

It took awhile to come about, however. In the years before fame came his way, he was known only by his real name, Reginald Kenneth Dwight. Born in Middlesex, England, he took up piano and the organ in his early teens and later studied on a scholarship at the Royal Academy of Music. His first job in the music business, however, was as a saloon piano player. That lasted only briefly, and then he channeled all his efforts into Rock.

The year was 1966, and he was 19 years old. The group was called Bluesology, and was controlled by bluesman Long John Baldry, who a few years earlier had helped Rod Stewart launch his career. After two years with Baldry, Reginald Kenneth Dwight decided it was time for a change, so he branched out on his own and adopted a fresh new name — Elton John.

His act and image were a carefully drawn composite, involving outlandish costumes (replete with characteristic glasses), a hyperactive performance which involved a variety of gymnastics while he played the piano, and music that for the most part was his creation alone. Helping him, however, was lyricist Bernie Taupin, who over the years would be an integral and important part of the Elton John act.

Acclaim was found first in his native England, but it quickly spread to the United States. He toured extensively in those early days, and many Rock critics have noted the substantial contributions that made to his early success because the Elton John performance was in itself such a singular visual sensation. Whichever way it came about, the fact was that from 1971 on Elton John's name was a regular sight on the Charts.

The discography that Elton John has accumulated during the 1970s reads like a compendium of the most immediately recognizable titles in Rock music, familiar to anyone who has even occasionally tuned in the Rock radio stations. The gold and platinum certifications have been numerous, and so has the critical appreciation.

In 1977, Elton John rather suddenly announced that he was retiring from the business. Too much too soon, he said; too demanding to keep up at his present pace. But, by 1978, his retirement was over and he was back on stage, in the studio, and right back up at the top of the Charts.

Today, Elton John and his image are a standard part of the popular entertainment scene throughout the world. He even has the dubious honor of being sculpted in wax and on display at Madame Toussaud's in London.

Kansas

Scorecard

Platinum Albums 2
Gold Albums 4
Gold Singles 1

Top Albums

Kansas (1974)
Song from America (1975)
*Masque** (1975)
*Leftoverture*** (1976)
*Point of Know Return** (1977)
*Two for the Show** (1978)

Memorable Singles

Can I Tell You (1974)
The Pilgrammage (1974)
Lonely Wind (1974)
Bringing It Back (1974)
Song for America (1975)
It's You (1976)
It Takes a Woman's Love (1976)
Carry On, Wayward Son (1976)
Questions of My Childhood (1976)
What's On My Mind (1977)
Lonely Street (1977)
*Dust in the Wind** (1978)
Magnum Opus (1978)

Current Recording Label: Kirschner
Records (distributed by Epic)

** Platinum Certification
 * Gold Certification

Kerry Livgren — *Guitar, Keyboards*
Steve Walsh — *Vocals, Keyboards, Vibes*
Phil Ehart — *Drums*
Dave Hope — *Bass*
Robbie Steinhardt — *Vocals, Violin*
Rich Williams — *Guitar*

There is not as much written about Kansas as there is about most other bands of their stature for the simple reason that the members of Kansas do not like to submit to press interviews and, as a matter of course, shun publicity as best they can. Steve Walsh gave one reason: "We just try to keep it to the music. The fans already know what we're all about."

Another way that they differ from many Rock groups today, too, is their behavior on stage. Kerry Livgren explained that to one Rock critic: "We refuse to obscure our music with garish on-stage theatrics."

Despite the down play of their image and stage actions, Kansas is today one of the most widely acclaimed groups in the business. They record and reap gold and often platinum certification; they tour and the halls and stadiums are sold out; they are, simply stated, a duly established star-group who no longer has to prove anything to anyone.

It began for the group back in the early 1970s in Topeka, the sedate, prairie-land capital of Kansas. That's where former high school classmates Kerry Livgren, Dave Hope, and Phil Ehart first formed a group with aspirations beyond merely entertaining at local school functions and named it after their home state. All of today's members of Kansas, according to a group spokesman, were in fact "born, raised, and raised hell in the midwest." It was not all that easy, however, trying to launch a successful Rock group in mid-America during those early years. After awhile, the originals split up, went their own ways (some formed a short-lived group called White Clover), and eventually came back together at the urging and organizing of drummer Phil Ehart. They decided to revive the name Kansas and give it another try.

Their first demo tape brought them into contact with promoter Don Kirschner, an entrepreneur who at one point had guided the Monkees to popular success. It was a fateful meeting. Their first album was released in March, 1974, and Kansas became an integral part of Rock history as a result of it.

Phil Ehart once said of the group: "This band is your basic small-town soap opera." As it has turned out, however, it is a small-town success story whose message and identity has spread far beyond even the confines of the nation of their citizenship. Kansas is an international celebrity today.

The music of Kansas has never been a regional phenomenon either. The group has always created music that has been described as a unique blend of American rhythms and British rock — the result defined as progressive rock, and Kansas is widely accepted as among the very best today in that genre.

Carole King

Scorecard

Gold Albums 8
Gold Singles 1
Grammy Awards 4

Top Albums

Carole King; Writer(1970)
Tapestry* (1971)
Music* (1971)
Rhymes and Reason* (1972)
Fantasy* (1973)
Wrap Around Joy* (1974)
Thoroughbred* (1975)
Simple Things* (1977)
Welcome Home (1978)
Carole King . . . Her Greatest Hits*
 (1978)

Memorable Singles

It Might as well Rain Until September
 (1962)
It's Too Late* (1971)
I Feel the Earth Move (1971)
You've Got a Friend (1971)
Hard Rock Cafe (1977)

Grammy Awards

1971 Album of the Year: Tapestry
 Record of the Year: It's Too Late
 Song of the Year: You've Got a
 Friend
 Best Pop Vocal Performance,
 Female: Tapestry

Current Recording Label:

Capitol Records

* Gold Certification

Carole King is another Brooklynite who emerged from that New York borough to make it big in the world of Pop/Rock (Barbra Streisand and Neil Diamond are among the other products of that city). King, however, established herself first as a songwriter, later as a performer; in both categories she now stands as one of the most respected figures in the industry.

Carole King began writing songs while she was still in high school. Before she was out of her teens, she married lyricist Gerry Goffin and the two set about trying to earn a living by writing songs. And they managed to do just that — practically from the first song they composed together.

During the early and middle 1960s, the team of King and Goffin became one of the most influential sources of songs on the American Rock scene, and they were booked solidly to compose for the top talents of the day. Among the Chart songs they produced during those years were: Natural Woman for Aretha Franklin; Hi-De-Ho for Blood, Sweat and Tears; Some Kind of Wonderful for the Drifters; Just Once in My Life for the Righteous Brothers; and their very first major hit Will You Still Love Me Tomorrow for the Shirelles.

Later in the 1960s, however, Carole King and Gerry Goffin split, both professionally and matrimonially. Carole moved to Los Angeles and began writing songs on her own. The urge to perform herself was always in the background. So, in 1968, she formed a trio with Danny Kortchmar and Charles Larkey and called it The City.

The group lasted a year, and when it dissolved Carole King took to playing back-up piano for the then skyrocketing Rock talent of James Taylor. He urged her, however, to strike out on her own. She decided it was worth a try.

Carole King tested her act and the audience reaction to it in several small clubs on the West Coast. Her album debut as a soloist was on the Ode label. Carole King: Writer was the title and it was well-received enough, at least critically if not at the record store counters, to encourage her to continue on her own.

Her second album, Tapestry, was released in 1971 and quickly rose on the Charts — it stayed there for a total of six years, becoming one of the most successful single LPs in the history of Pop/Rock. The album and the songs from it also earned four Grammy awards that year for Carole King.

Albums and singles rolled steadily after that, so did the awards and the worldwide recognition. Like all the other Rock stars of her stature, Carole King has toured extensively to sell-out crowds and a dedicated, almost cult-like following. In 1977, she moved from Ode to Capitol Records where she formed her own label, Avatar. Today, Carole King still reigns as one of the single most respected singer-songwriters in the entire Pop/Rock world.

Kiss

Scorecard

Platinum Albums (as a group)–5
Platinum Albums (as individuals)— 4
Gold Albums (as a group)—9
Gold Albums (as individuals)—4
Gold Singles—1

Top Albums

*Kiss** (1974)
*Hotter Than Hell** (1974)
*Dressed to Kill** (1975)
*Alive** (1975)
*Destroyer*** (1976)
The Originals (1976)
*Rock and Roll Over*** (1976)
*Love Gun*** (1977)
*Kiss Alive*** (1977)
*Double Platinum*** (1978)

Memorable Singles

Let Me Go (1975)
Rock and Roll All Night (1975)
C'mon and Love Me (1975)
Shout It Out Loud (1976)
Flaming Youth (1976)
*Beth** (1976)
Detroit Rock City (1976)
Hard Luck Woman (1976)
Calling Dr. Love (1977)

Solo Albums

*Gene Simmons*** (1978)
*Ace Frehley*** (1978)
*Paul Stanley** (1978)
*Peter Criss*** (1978)

Solo Singles

New York Groove (Ace Frehley) (1978)
Radioactive (Gene Simmons) (1978)
Hold Me, Touch Me (Paul Stanley) (1978)

Current Recording Label: Casablanca

** Platinum Certification
 * Gold Certification

Gene Simmons — *Vocals, Bass*
Paul Stanley — *Guitar*

Peter Criss — *Drums*
Ace Frehley — *Guitar*

Blood oozing from one mouth, flames leaping out from another, nightmarishly painted faces, straggly wigs, high-heel dragon boots, jump suits and chains, and a general atmosphere of *dementia praecox* paints a verbal picture of the visual extravaganza we have come to know as Kiss.

Kiss is the brainchild of Gene Simmons and Paul Stanley, who founded the group back in 1973. Peter Criss and Ace Frehley survived the auditions the two founders held and the group unveiled its macabre musical act the same year. "Outrageous," one critic called it and stalked out of the performance. Another writer suggested, "The rock press had a collectivce attack of the dry heaves."

Kiss, however, persisted and eventually prevailed. Their growing legion of followers were not chagrined by the strange combination of horror and lunacy that marked their performances, instead they were caught up in it and with the music that Kiss managed to produce amid all the bedlam. Less than two years after their inaugural appearance, the group posted its first album certified gold, *Dressed to Kill.*

The group also became popular enough to transcend ordinary rock exposure. There was a movie — *KISS Meets the Phantom* — to showcase their talents. There was also a comic book that featured them in the same extraordinary heroics usually associated with super-heroes like Batman or Spiderman (no other rock group can claim this distinction).

Behind those painted faces, however, lurk four distinct human beings. Gene Simmons, said to be seven feet tall in his specially-made high heels, is a great fan of horror movies and once was a member of the Count Dracula Society. He is also an avid collector of rings, buckles, bracelets, insects, and spiders.

Paul Stanley, on the other hand, is described as being like "the boy next door," but next door to whom has never been clearly defined. He says his closest interests after music are swimming, wrestling, playing football, and driving his silver and burgundy Rolls Royce.

Peter Criss is a tinkerer around the house and likes to throw an occasional dart or two, which he claims keeps his drumming muscles in shape.

Ace Frehley's outside interests include pinball, pachinko, and buying toys in Japan. His ambition, he said, is to pilot his own rocketship before he gets older.

As a group, Kiss' popularity is at its zenith today. The four members are also soaring as individual performers. In 1978, each member recorded his own solo album and all of them landed on the charts simultaneously. No other group in rock history has done that, but then no other group in rock history has been anything quite like Kiss.

Barry Manilow

Scorecard

Platinum Albums — 4
Gold Albums — 7
Gold Singles — 5
Grammy Awards — 1

Top Albums

*Barry Manilow** (1973)
*Barry Manilow II** (1974)
*Tryin' to Get the Feeling** (1975)
*This One's for You*** (1976)
*Barry Manilow Live*** (1976)
*Even Now*** (1977)
*Barry Manilow's Greatest Hits*** (1978)

Memorable Singles

*Mandy** (1974)
It's a Miracle (1975)
Could It Be Magic (1975)
*I Write the Songs** (1975)
Looks Like We Made It (1976)
Tryin' to Get the Feeling (1976)
This One's for You (1976)
Weekend in New England (1976)
Daybreak (1977)
*Can't Smile Without You** (1977)
Even Now (1978)
*Copacabana** (1978)
Somewhere in the Night (1978)

Grammy Awards

1978 Best Pop Vocal Performance,
Male: *Copacabana*

Current Recording Label: Arista

** Platinum Certification
* Gold Certification

In 1972, Bette Midler was getting her start by singing for the denizens of New York's Continental Baths. The young man accompanying her on the piano, an unknown singer, musician, and songwriter was Barry Manilow.

Manilow continued to provide accompaniment for Bette Midler in the months that followed and became her musical director, eventually co-producing her first album, *The Divine Miss M,* which was good enough to win a Grammy award. Barry Manilow then went on tour with her — on the condition, however, that he be permitted to introduce several of his own songs at each performance. It was agreed, and he took the spot of opening the second act each night. It was his first large step forward as a performer.

Barry Manilow had, in fact, been a musician for quite a few years. Back in Brooklyn, where he grew up, he played the accordion when he was seven, the piano at 13, and attended the New York College of Music at 19. During those college-age years, he lived in an apartment in Greenwich Village and worked as a mail boy for CBS. At one point, he was given the chance to write the music for an off-Broadway show called *The Drunkard,* which turned out to be a critical success. After that, there was a stint with a female singer, but the duo never did much more than play a few small clubs. Then came the Baths and Bette Midler.

When Barry Manilow set off on his own in 1974, he had almost no following and little in the way of credentials — his one album, just released, was making hardly a ripple on the Pop/Rock sea. Late that year however, he came out with the single *Mandy.* Suddenly everyone knew the name and voice of Barry Manilow as the record moved swiftly to the top of the Charts and gold record certification. It was the beginning of an incredible streak of 12 successive singles that would land in the Top Ten. The albums that also flowed from the presses were measured in sales of several million each. At one point in 1977, all *five* of his albums were on the charts — only two other performers had ever done that before, Frank Sinatra and Johnny Mathis.

One writer explained the phenomenon this way: "Manilow has emerged as one of those few entertainers with wide and varying appeal to many of all age groups. He transcends the high walls between tastes of generations."

With the record industry in tow, Barry Manilow moved into New York's legitimate theatre district in 1976 with his show *Barry Manilow on Broadway* — SRO for every performance and was awarded a special Tony award. The following year, it was television. *The Barry Manilow Special* was aired nationally on ABC-TV in March 1977, and at the end of the year it was awarded an Emmy for Outstanding Musical Variety Special of the Year.

Barry Manilow, it can be safely said, has come a long way from the Continental Baths in 1972 New York.

Scorecard

Platinum Albums — 4
Gold Albums — 10
Gold Singles — 7
Grammy Awards — 4

Top Albums

McCartney* (1970)
Ram* (1971)
Wings Wild Life* (1971)
Red Rose Speedway* (1973)
Band on the Run* (1973)
Venus and Mars* (1975)
Wings at the Speed of Sound** (1976)
Wings Over America** (1976)
London Town** (1978)
Wings Greatest** (1978)

Memorable Singles

Another Day (1971)
Uncle Albert-Admiral Halsey* (1971)
Give Ireland Back to the Irish (1972)
Mary Had a Little Lamb (1972)
HI, HI, HI (1972)
My Love* (1973)
Live and Let Die* (1973)
Helen Wheels (1973)
Jet (1973)
Band on the Run* (1973)
Listen to What the Man Said* (1975)
Letting Go (1975)
Venus and Mars Rock Show (1975)
Silly Love Songs* (1976)
Let 'Em In* (1976)
London Town (1978)

Grammy Awards

1966 Song of the Year: Michelle
      Best Contemporary Solo: Eleanor
      Rigby
1971 Best Accompaniment and Arrange-
      ment: Uncle Albert-Admiral
      Halsey
1974 Best Pop Vocal Group Album:
      Band on the Run

Current Recording Label: Capitol

** Platinum Certification
 * Gold Certification

Paul McCartney & Wings

The break-up of the Beatles came along with the dawn of the 1970s. Bitterly, the members of the most internationally famous and financially successful music group of all time moved out on their own. Selected by many as the man most likely to succeed in that effort was Paul McCartney because of the very rich and very visible talents he possessed in areas of both performance and songwriting.

The release of Uncle Albert-Admiral Halsey the following year lent a bit of credence to that assumption. The flow of gold records, Grammy awards and critical praise that followed has cemented it. None of the other former Beatles can claim the accomplishments and acceptance that Paul McCartney has managed to register throughout the world during the past eight years.

Wings was born as a result of the death of the Beatles. The first member signed on was McCartney's wife (of only a little more than a year at that time), Linda. Since then, she has remained while a number of other musicians have come and gone. The core of Wings, of course, is McCartney; the others have always been labeled as contributing talents.

By 1973, Paul McCartney and Wings were fully established. Band on the Run was a glorious success as a single and an album, and McCartney took his group on their first tour of England. That year he also produced a major television special for viewing there as well as in America. And it was also the year that he began his "moveable recording studio," which started with a jaunt to Nigeria to record Band on the Run and has made its way through several other countries since, perhaps culminating with their most recent album London Town when it was cut on a chartered yacht in the Virgin Islands.

Paul McCartney brought Wings to the United States back in 1976 as part of a world-wide tour. It was one of the most successful in recent rock history.

The group today is a trio. Paul, Linda and Denny Laine (who has also remained from the very beginning). Success has come, so have the material rewards that accompany it in the rock world. That, however, is only part of it, according to Paul McCartney — what it's really all about: "It's down to whether you like music or not. And the stuff we're doing now, we like." So apparently do quite a few million other people today.

Olivia Newton-John

Scorecard

Platinum Albums — 3
Platinum Singles — 1
Gold Albums — 9
Gold Singles — 8
Grammy Awards — 3

Top Albums

*Let Me Be There** (1973)
*If You Love Me, Let Me Know** (1974)
*Have You Never Been Mellow** (1975)
*Clearly Love** (1975)
*Come On Over** (1976)
*Don't Stop Believin'** (1976)
Making a Good Thing Better (1977)
*Greatest Hits*** (1977)
Grease (Soundtrack)** (1978)
*Totally Hot*** (1978)

Memorable Singles

If Not for You (1971)
It's So Hard to Say Goodbye (1971)
What is Life (1972)
Just a Little Too Much (1972)
Take Me Home Country Roads (1973)
*Let Me Be There** (1973)
*If You Love Me, Let Me Know** (1974)
*I Honestly Love You** (1974)
*Have You Never Been Mellow** (1975)
*Please, Mister, Please** (1975)
Something Better to Do (1975)
Let It Shine (1975)
Come on Over (1976)
Every Face Tells a Story (1976)
Don't Stop Believin' (1976)
Sam (1977)
Making a Good Thing Better (1977)
*You're the One That I Want*** (1978)
*Summer Nights** (1978)
*Hopelessly Devoted to You** (1978)
A Little More Love (1978)

Current Recording Label: MCA Records

** Platinum Certification
 * Gold Certification

The girl with the very round, expressive eyes who lives by the Pacific Ocean in southern California with the six horses, four dogs, and two cats is no relationship whatever to Wayne Newton or Elton John. She is, in fact, the daughter of a scholar and former headmaster of a college in Australia and the granddaughter of a Nobel prize winning German physicist (Max Born).

Olivia Newton-John was born in Cambridge, England, but grew up in Melbourne, Australia, where early in her life she decided to forge a career in music. At about 13 years old, she formed a group with three other girls and began performing under the name of Sol Four. When she was 15, the group had dissolved, but Olivia tried a solo in a talent contest that offered the first prize of a trip back to England. She won it, and that was the real beginning or her singing career. It was also her farewell to Australia.

In England, Olivia sang with another Australian girl, Pat Carroll, for two years; then she struck out on her own. Her debut on the American music scene came in 1973, and she was an instant success. Her first record in the United States, *Let Me Be There,* was certified gold and won for her a Grammy in the Country Vocal category.

1974 brought two more Grammy awards and a rainfall of other tributes:

No. 1 Award for LPs and singles — *Billboard*
No. 1 Female Vocalist, singles and albums — *Cashbox*
Favorite Female Vocalist, Pop/Rock — *American Music Award*
Favorite Female Vocalist, Country — *American Music Award*
Top Female Vocalist of the Year — *Country Music*
Rising Star of the Year — *AGVA*
Top Female Vocalist, singles and albums — *Record World*
Favorite Female Musical Performer — *People's Choice*
Female Artist of the Year — *Bobby Poe's Pop Music Award*

Since she came to the United States, Olivia Newton-John has been in the rock universe a star of the highest magnitude. Her tours of the country have always been sell-out affairs; her records have sold in the multi-millions. Her first movie role, as Sandy in the musical *Grease,* in which she co-starred with John Travolta, was another extraordinary chapter in her story of success. *Grease* also provided her with a total of three single records that each have earned gold certification.

Today, Olivia Newton-John is one of the most sought-after talents in America in every music performance medium — recordings, the live stage, television, and motion pictures.

Scorecard

Platinum Albums 2
Gold Albums 22
Gold Singles 5

Top Albums

The Rolling Stones (1964)
The Rolling Stones Now (1965)
Now (1965)
*Out of Our Heads** (1965)
*December's Children** (1965)
*Big Hits** (1966)
*Aftermath** (1966)
*Got "Live" If You Want It** (1966)
*Between the Buttons** (1967)
*Flowers** (1967)
*Their Satanic Majesties Request** (1967)
*Beggar's Banquet** (1968)
*Through the Past Darkly** (1969)
*Let It Bleed** (1969)
*Get Your Ya-Ya's Out** (1970)
*Sticky Fingers** (1971)
*Hot Rocks 1964 — 1971** (1971)
*Exile on Main Street** (1972)
*More Hot Rocks** (1972)
*Goat's Head Soup** (1973)
*It's Only Rock and Roll** (1974)
*Made in the Shade** (1975)
*Black and Blue*** (1976)
*Love You Live** (1977)
*Some Girls*** (1978)

Memorable Singles

Not Fade Away (1964)
Time Is on My Side (1964)
The Last Time (1965)
*I Can't Get No Satisfaction** (1965)
Get Off My Cloud (1965)
As Tears Go By (1965)
19th Nervous Breakdown (1966)
Paint It Black (1966)
Mother's Little Helper (1966)
Lady Jane (1966)
*Ruby Tuesday** (1966)
We Love You (1967)
She's A Rainbow (1967)
Jumpin' Jack Flash (1968)
Street Fighting Man (1968)
*Honky Tonk Women** (1969)
You Can't Always Get What You Want
 (1969)
Brown Sugar (1971)
Tumbling Dice (1972)
Happy (1972)
*Angie** (1973)
Doo Doo Doo Doo Doo (Heartbreaker)
 (1973)
It's Only Rock 'n' Roll (1974)
Ain't Too Proud to Beg (1974)
Fool to Cry (1976)
Hot Stuff (1976)
*Miss You*** (1978)
Shattered (1978)

Current Recording Label: Rolling
 Stones Records (distributed by
 Atlantic

** Platinum Certification
 * Gold Certification

The Rolling Stones

Mick Jagger — *Lead Vocals, Harmonica*
Keith Richard — *Lead Guitar, Vocals*
Bill Wyman — *Bass*

Charlie Watts — *Drums*
Ron Wood — *Guitar*

For more than 15 raucous years, the Rolling Stones have enjoyed the ultimate prestige in Rock and Roll. The group has at the same time survived drug busts, controversial deaths associated with them (one within the group, the other at one of their performances), censorship, kidnapping threats, and the ever-changing tastes of Rock audiences. Mick Jagger, Keith Richard, Bill Wyman, and Charlie Watts were all there at the very beginning back in 1962. So was rhythm guitarist Brian Jones, but he had horrendous problems with drugs, enough to force him to drop out of the group in 1969. (Later the same year, he was found dead at the bottom of his swimming pool, the victim, according to the coroner's report, of a "misadventure.")

The Rolling Stones were a hit from the very first album. But the reactions to them were diverse, to say the least. The "raunchiness and arrogance of their music," is the way one Rock critic in 1963 described their output; that, along with their hyperkinetic stage performances, the outrageousness of their rebellion, their obviously total lack of inhibition or restraint was all new to the Rock world of the early 1960s.

The core of the Stones has always been Mick Jagger, son of a schoolmaster and a one-time student at the London School of Economics, and Keith Richard, the superb stylist and song writer. One writer referred to them as "Richard the musician and Jagger the showman who complement each other perfectly."

The Rolling Stone tours have always been something else — expeditions, trials of logistics, multi-million dollar experiences. And they, too, have not been without their controversy. At one, held at a raceway just outside San Francisco in 1969, the members of Hell's Angels motorcycle gang who were hired as guards to protect the Stones while they were performing beat and stabbed a youth to death when he ventured too close to the stage.

For a tour today, the Stones will charter a large Boeing jet to transport themselves and a supporting cast of about 30 others. They will lease a convoy of at least a dozen trucks to cart around the 22 tons of lighting and sound equipment they use as well as Mick Jagger's $75,000 wardrobe, Keith Richard's 20 guitars, and various other pieces of paraphernalia. They will hire maybe 30 or so stagehands in each city they visit on the tour and other local support troops. But the gross revenue from a single tour is normally in excess of $10 million, sometimes far in excess of it. No one has ever worried about the Rolling Stones making out well in the dollars and cents category.

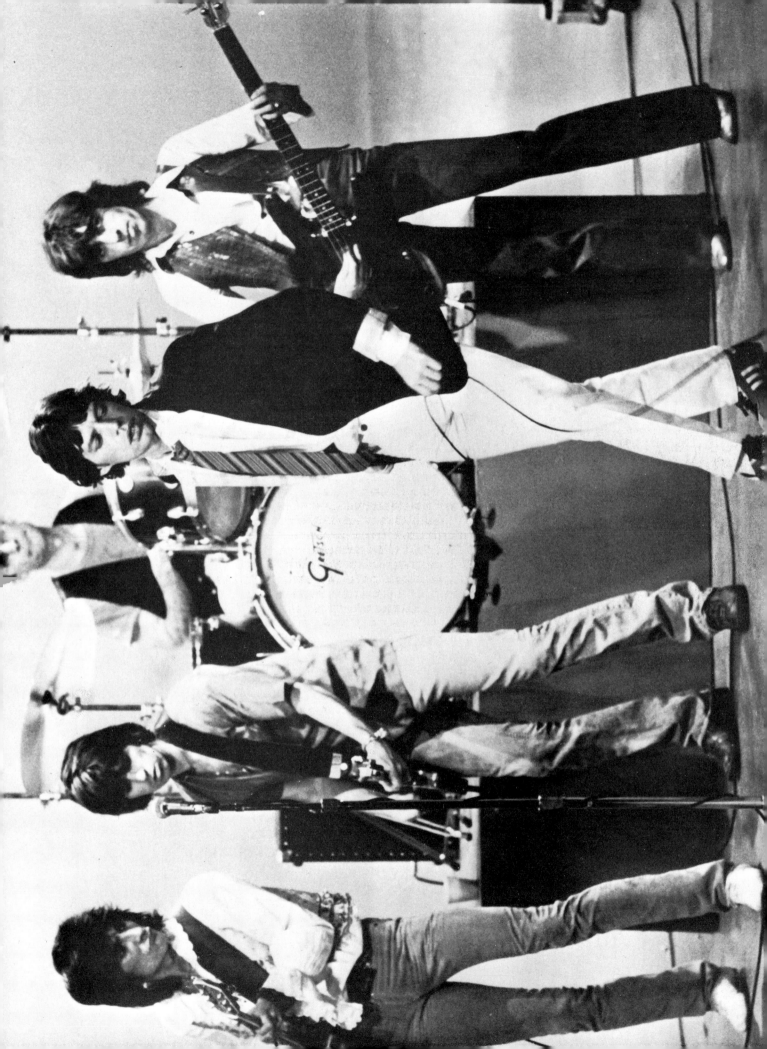

Linda Ronstadt

Scorecard

Platinum Albums — 4
Gold Albums — 8
Gold Singles — 2
Grammy Awards — 2

Top Albums

*The Stone Poneys Featuring Linda
  Ronstadt* (1967)
Stone Poneys Evergreen, Vol. 2 (1967)
*Linda Ronstadt: Stone Poneys &
  Friends, Vol. 3* (1968)
Hand Sown . . . Home Grown (1969)
Silk Purse (1970)
Linda Ronstadt (1972)
*Don't Cry Now** (1973)
Different Drum (1974)
*Heart Like A Wheel** (1974)
*Prisoner in Disguise** (1975)
*Hasten Down the Wind*** (1976)
*Greatest Hits*** (1976)
*A Retrospective** (1977)
*Simple Dreams*** (1977)
*Living in the U.S.A.*** (1978)

Memorable Singles

The Long Way Around (1969)
Will You Love Me Tomorrow (1970)
Long, Long Time (1970)
She's a Very Lovely Woman (1970)
Can It Be True (1971)
Rock Me on the Water (1972)
I Can Almost See It (1973)
Love Has No Pride (1973)
Silver Threads and Golden Needles
  (1974)
Colorado (1974)
You're No Good (1974)
I Can't Help It (1974)
When Will I Be Loved (1975)
It Doesn't Matter Anymore (1975)
Love Is a Rose (1975)
Heat Wave (1975)
Tracks of My Tears (1975)
That Will Be the Day (1976)
Someone to Lay Down Beside Me
  (1976)
Lose Again (1977)
*Blue Bayou** (1977)
It's So Easy (1977)
Ooh Baby Baby (1978)

Grammy Awards

1975 Best Country Vocal Performance,
     Female: *I Can't Help It*
1976 Best Pop Vocal Performance,
     Female: *Hasten Down the Wind*

Current Recording Label: Asylum

** Platinum Certification
 * Gold Certification

The Linda Ronstadt of the early 1970s was noted more for her barefoot, braless, tight-jeaned stage presence than the quality of what she rendered musically. The Linda Ronstadt of the late 1970s, on the other hand, is a demure young lady photographed in dresses, with the focus of attention on her soft sometimes sad eyes instead of other body parts, one who is said to keep occasional company with the governor of California, and the winner of various Grammy nominations and awards.

The transition was a major one. But the appreciation of her singing talents was a well-founded one, even if it was a long time in coming.

Linda Ronstadt, who was born and raised in Tucson, Arizonia, dropped out of the University of Arizona after her freshman year and headed for Los Angeles with a dream of making it in the Pop/Rock world. The year was 1964 and she was 18 years old at the time. In LA she formed her first group with two musicians, Bob Kimmel and Kenny Edwards. They called themselves the Stone Poneys.

With the Stone Poneys, Linda Ronstadt cut three albums on the Capitol label but none of them drew much attention. The Stone Poneys, after five years of playing small clubs and other local gigs, weren't getting anywhere. So, in 1969, Linda moved out on her own with a solo album, *Hand Sown . . . Home Grown*. It did not do much better than the Stone Poneys' efforts.

In 1971, however, things began to change for the better. First, she organized a new band that headlined Glenn Frey, Don Henley, and Randy Meisner — three superb musicians who would later form their own group, The Eagles, and rise to the top of the Charts themselves. The new output of records were now selling much better for Linda Ronstadt and her name was becoming more widely known.

In 1974, the single *You're No Good* reached No. 1 on the Charts, and Linda Ronstadt had finally made it to the top, ten full years after she first left Arizona to give the business a try. The following year, she cemented her repuatation as a fine singer by walking off with her first Grammy award for *I Can't Help It (If I'm Still in Love With You)*.

By 1977, her image was totally transformed. Success had bred a sedate, manicured Linda Ronstadt, whose professional touch was a unique blend of gold and platinum when it came to making records. She appeared on the cover of Time magazine that year as well as People and Rolling Stone, and the Playboy Poll named her the Top Female Singer in both pop and country categories.

Her album *Simple Dreams* sold more than 3½ million copies in less than a year's time. By 1979, Linda Ronstadt, after 15 years in the business, was securely at the top of it — providing some very good music as well as some provocative and lingering memories of the Linda Ronstadt of the past.

Todd Rundgren

Scorecard

Gold Albums — 1

Top Albums

Runt (1971)
*Something/Anything** (1972)
A Wizard, A True Star (1973)
Todd (1973)
Utopia (1974)
Initiation (1975)
Another Live . . . Utopia (1975)
Faithful (1976)
Ra (1976)
Ooops! Wrong Planet (1977)
Back to the Bars (1978)

Memorable Singles

I Saw the Light (1970)
Be Nice to Me (1971)
A Long Time, A Long Way to Go (1971)
I Saw the Light (remake) (1972)
Couldn't I Just Tell You (1972)
Wolfman Jack (1972)
Hello, Its Me (1972)
We Got to Get You a Woman (1972)
Sometimes I Don't Know What to Feel
    (1973)
Does Anybody Love You (1973)
A Dream Goes On Forever (1974)
Heavy Metal Kids (1974)
Real Man (1975)

Current Recording Label: Warner Bros.

* Gold Certification

His music has been described by one rock critic as "futuristic synthesized space meanderings spun around soul-influenced accessible backbeats." Todd Rundgren might agree with that — then again, he might not. "I just put on what I think sounds good," he once said, but then added: "What sounds good to me though might be too much for somebody else . . . Anyway, at what point does the noise end and the music begin? At what point does sight end and sound begin? The lines get blurrier and blurrier all the time." That really says something about the music associated with Todd Rundgren today.

To say Todd Rundgren and his cortege called Utopia are unique is an exercise in understatement. Their presence on stage and the music they unleash are original in the truest sense of the word. That, however, is something Todd Rundgren has strived for ever since the early 1970s when he set about changing the entire style of the music he was writing and the way he was performing it.

Rundgren's career actually goes back to the late 1960s when as a teenager he performed with a small band called Woody's Truckstop in his hometown of Philadelphia. At the end of that decade, he hooked up with another Philadelphia-based group called Nazz and toured much of the U.S. east coast. It was the same year he cut the single *Hello, Its Me,* which quickly rose to the top of the Charts and introduced the name Todd Rundgren to Pop/Rock fans throughout the nation. With that, he set out on his own in earnest.

His talents, even in those early days, were multi-faceted. He was not merely a singer who normally accompanied himself on the guitar; he was also a songwriter, an accomplished player of various other musical instruments besides the guitar, an arranger, a band leader, a sound engineer, and a record producer. Rundgren exhibited clear evidence of his expertise in all these facets of the music business during his stratospheric career in the 1970s. (As an engineer/producer, for example, he worked with many of the country's top rock names, including American Dream, Paul Butterfield, Grand Funk Railroad, and Meat Loaf.)

The real change in Todd Rundgren's musical style and the new goals he set for himself in the Pop/Rock world came about 1973. That was around the time he was gathering up the members of Utopia in order to help him achieve a new and more meaningful form of rock music. An innovative, Rundgren-conceived musical imagery was introduced more or less in the autumn of 1974 when the album *Utopia* was released. The style and depth have remained, been refined, and broadened in scope during the ensuing years. His following today is large and very serious and, at least so far, totally unwavering in its dedication.

Santana

Scorecard

Gold Albums —12

Top Albums

Santana* (1969)
Abraxas* (1970)
Santana* (1971)
Caravanserai* (1972)
Carlos Santana & Buddy Miles Live* (1973)
Welcome* (1973)
Love, Devotion, Surrender* (1973)
Greatest Hits* (1974)
Borboletta (1974)
Amigos* (1976)
Festival* (1977)
Moonflower* (1977)
Inner Secrets* (1978)

Memorable Singles

Jingo (1969)
Evil Ways (1969)
Black Magic Woman (1970)
Oye Coma Va (1971)
Everybody's Everything (1971)
No One to Depend On (1972)
All the Love in the Universe (1972)
Just in Time to See the Sun (1973)
When I Look into Your Eyes (1974)
Samba De Sausalito (1974)
Mirage (1974)
Give and Take (1975)
Let It Shine (1976)
Dance Sister Dance (1976)
Europa (1976)
Take Me with You (1976)
Let the Children Play (1977)
Give Me Love (1977)
Revelations (1977)
Stormy (1978)

Current Recording Label:
Columbia Records

* Gold Certification

Carlos Santana — *Lead Guitar, Vocals*
Greg Walker — *Lead Vocals*
Graham Lear — *Drums*
Chris Rhyne — *Keyboards, Synthesizer*
Raul Rekow — *Bongos, Congas*
Armando Peraza — *Percussion*
Pete Escovedo — *Timbales*
David Margen — *Bass*
Chris Solberg — *Rhythm Guitar*

At Woodstock, the now-famous rock festival held in upstate New York back in August 1969, one of the single biggest hits to play before the half-million Rock fans who gathered there was a relatively unknown group called the Santana Blues Band. The group had just released their first album earlier that month but it had barely reached the record store shelves by the time of the festival much less the ears of those who might have wanted to listen to it. Its timing, however, coincident with Woodstock, could not have been better.

Carlos Santana, the son of a mariachi musician, was the founder and leader of the group. Born in Mexico, he had moved up to San Francisco in the mid-1960s to join the creative Rock scene that was burgeoning there in those days. He brought his own approach, a very original one that essentially was, as one Rock writer described it: "Musical explorations into the world of Latin, rock, jazz, rhythm & blues, and acoustic and electric rock."

Santana gathered a core group back in the 60s, but all of them have since gone their separate ways. The group members who back up Santana today have signed on since 1976, with the single exception of percussionist Armando Peraza who has been with Santana since the early 70s.

Santana followed Woodstock and his first album *Santana* with another smash album, *Abraxas*, and the two best-selling singles: *Evil Ways* and *Black Magic Woman*. It was more than enough to solidify his place in the upper stratum of Rock recognition. Santana also took to the road — personal appearance was a trademark he wanted associated with the group that bore his name — and in the years that followed they achieved the reputation of being the single most extensive touring band in the business. In the 70s, Santana has performed in practically every major city in the United States and traveled the world — Europe, Japan, Australia, Southeast Asia, Central America, and South America.

In the early years of this decade, Santana also underwent his own "personal discovery," as he called it, and re-styled his music as well as his personal life. He took to an Eastern philosophy, and his music became a deeper, more introspective one, much different from the admixture of Latin and Rock that he had created before. Later, however, he returned to the musical form he had pioneered and with it came an even more mature blending of Rock, rhythm & blues, and lyrical Latin music.

Bob Seger & the Silver Bullet Band

Bob Seger — *Lead vocals*
Drew Abbott — *Guitars*
Robyn Robbins — *Keyboards*
Alto Reed — *Horns*
Chris Campbell — *Bass*
David Teegarden — *Percusssion*

Scorecard

Platinum Albums — 3
Gold Albums — 3

Top Albums

Ramblin' Gamblin' Man (1968)
Noah (1969)
Mongrel (1970)
Brand New Morning (1971)
Smokin' O.P.s (1972)
Back in '72 (1973)
Bob Seger Seven (1974)
Beautiful Loser (1975)
*Live Bullet*** (1976)
*Night Moves*** (1976)
*Stranger in Town*** (1978)

Memorable Singles

Ramblin' Gamblin' Man (1968)
Ivory (1969)
Noah (1969)
Lucifer (1970)
Lookin' Back (1971)
Turn on Your Love Light (1972)
Rosalie (1973)
Need Ya (1973)
Get Out of Denver (1974)
UMC (1974)
Beautiful Loser (1975)
Travelin' Man (1975)
Nutbush City Limits (1975)
Night Moves (1976)
Main Street (1977)
Rock and Roll Never Forgets (1977)
We've Got Tonight (1978)

Current Recording Label: Capitol
Records

** Platinum Certification
 * Gold Certification

Bob Seger made it big in 1976 . . . finally, but it took 15 years for him to do it. After the recognition came, he observed, "It was a long hard road to the top, a road full of potholes and sleepless nights. There never was a convenient road map."

For most of the 15 years he spent working at the professions of songwriter, singer, and musician, it appeared that Bob Seger might never break out onto the national scene, that he was doomed to be merely a regional cult hero, which in fact he grew into. He was born in Ann Arbor, Michigan, but his early success was in Detroit and its surrounding area.

Music and his own brand of creativity were the vehicles he used to escape the traps of the city streets that was the environment he was growing up in. He was 15 when he cut his first single record back in 1961 for a local record company in Michigan. Blues-rock was his specialty, and his version of it was well accepted, in Detroit anyway. He wrote his own music and it strongly illustrated the life he lived and observed in that city. One writer has said of Seger's compositions: "His songs reflect the anguish and the joy, the magnetism and the bewildering nature of long, lonely neon nights."

In the early days, he worked with different bands (the Silver Bullet Band of today did not join with him until the mid 1970s). His records continued to do well in the Detroit area, but it was not until 1969 that he achieved recognition on a national scale. That occured when the title single for his first album, *Ramblin' Gamblin' Man,* fought its way out of Michigan and onto the national charts.

Songs continued to flow from his pen, and new albums were cut over the next few years; still Seger was far from a national rock celebrity. It wasn't, in fact, until 1975 that he could claim that kind of status. It was after the Silver Bullet Band had been formed, that the nation took serious notice of Bob Seger and his new group.

In 1976, the album *Live Bullet* hit the market and within a half-year became Seger's first certified gold record. Two more best-selling albums and a bevy of top of the Chart singles solidified his position in today's highest echelon of rock stars.

In late 1977, Seger took his Silver Bullet Band out of the United States to establish its reputation in Europe. Three weeks and 14 performances later, the group was a well-known commodity in England, Scotland, France, and Germany. The regional rock-star had become an internationally accepted rock-artist.

Carly Simon

Scorecard

Platinum Albums — 1
Gold Albums — 5
Gold Singles — 3
Grammy Awards — 1

Top Albums

Carly Simon (1971)
*Anticipation** (1971)
*No Secrets** (1972)
*Hotcakes** (1974)
Playing Possum (1975)
*The Best of Carly Simon** (1975)
Another Passenger (1976)
*Boys in the Trees*** (1978)

Memorable Singles

*That's the Way I've Always Heard It
 Should Be* (1971)
Anticipation (1971)
Legend in Your Own Time (1972)
The Girl You Think You See (1972)
*You're So Vain** (1972)
The Right Thing To Do (1973)
*Mockingbird** (1974)
Haven't Got Time for the Pain (1974)
Attitude Dancing (1975)
Waterfall (1975)
More and More (1975)
It Keeps You Runnin' (1976)
Be With Me (1976)
Half a Chance (1976)
*Nobody Does It Better** (1977)

Grammy Awards

1971 Best New Artist of the Year

Current Recording Label: Elektra

** Platinum Certification
 * Gold Certification

The radio airwaves in early 1971 were suddenly inundated with a softly lyrical voice carrying the plaintive message in the song *That's the Way I've Always Heard It Should Be*. The singer was an unknown, the song was her first single. It would prove, however, to be Carly Simon's introduction to the top 20 and, in turn, to introduce Carly Simon to the tens of millions of people who listen to Pop/Rock music every day.

Carly Simon emerged from both a musical and literary family in New York City. Both of her parents were avid musical enthusiasts, a trait they consciously strove to pass on to their children, and her father, Richard Simon, was one of the Simons who lent the family name to the large New York publishing firm of Simon & Schuster.

Carly Simon began performing while she was still a student at Sarah Lawrence College, an affluent private school in Bronxville, New York. With her sister Lucy, they entertained with folk songs at a variety of school functions under the name the Simon Sisters. From their inauspicious beginning, she tried a few small club dates in the New York City area, which led to a collaboration with lyricist Jacob Brackman, who over the years would work with Carly on many of the top songs she would introduce.

In 1970, there was an offer of a recording contract from Elektra Records. Her first venture with them was her first album, *Carly Simon*, and, of course, its core hit, *That's the Way I've Always Heard It Should Be*.

The success of her first record album and single brought about the demand for her personal appearance, which meant live performances and touring (the latter being one of her least favorite activities in the business). Besides some solo work on various stages she also opened for Cat Stevens at the Troubador in Los Angeles and for Kris Kristoferson at the Bitter End in New York. By the end of 1972, however, she no longer had to open for anyone, she was a fully established performer herself, holder of several gold certifications, winner of a Grammy award, and one of the most sought-after vocalists in the country.

While all this was happening, she married fellow-rock star James Taylor. As a family (they now have several children), they have successfully guided three careers: his, hers, and their domestic one together.

Carly Simon herself has continued to turn out hit after hit — her 1977 single *Nobody Does It Better* was nominated both for a Grammy and an Oscar (it was the theme song for the James Bond movie *The Spy Who Loved Me*). Her presence is always captivating, but it is truly her music that has made her the superstar she is today: "Unique," one writer called it, "combining a spectrum of styles from pop to jazz with a touch of classical orchestration as well as folk and rock."

Cat Stevens

Scorecard

Gold Albums — 9

Top Albums

Matthew and Son (1967)
New Masters (1968)
*Mona Bone Jakon** (1970)
*Tea for the Tillerman** (1970)
*Teaser and the Firecat** (1970)
*Catch Bull at Four** (1972)
*Foreigner** (1973)
*Buddha and the Chocolate Box** (1974)
*Greatest Hits** (1975)
*Numbers** (1975)
*Izitso** (1977)
Back to Earth (1978)

Memorable Singles

I Love My Dog (1967)
Matthew and Son (1967)
Here Comes My Baby (1967)
I'm Gonna Get Me a Gun (1967)
A Bad Night (1967)
Lady D'Arbanville (1970)
Moon Shadow (1971)
Peace Train (1971)
Morning Has Broken (172)
Sitting (1972)
The Hurt (1972)
Oh, Very Young (1974)
Another Saturday Night (1974)
Ready (1974)
Two Fine People (1975)
Banapple Gas (1976)
Old School Yard (1977)

Current Recording Label: A & M
Records

* Gold Certification

Stephen Demetri Georgiou is his real name. His father was a Cypriot, his mother a Swede, and the family was living above a restaurant in London when he was born back in 1948. He decided a number of years later that Cat Stevens would be a more appropriate name for a rock singer.

He bought his first guitar at 15 while he was still thinking of making a career as a painter. The following year, Cat Stevens dropped out of art school and devoted his time to composing original songs and performing them. In those days of the mid-1960s, he developed an almost immediate following in England, and before Stevens was 20 years old he had cut his first album. His early singles soared into the British Top-20. He toured England and most of the rest of Europe. He had, as they say, arrived at a very early age.

Then everything came to a sudden stop. He contracted tuberculosis. Three months in a British hospital and another year of recuperation were required before Cat Stevens could return to the world of rock music.

While he convalesced, however, Cat Stevens also set about changing his musical style. His earlier songs had been too superficial, he said. He wanted more depth, more meaning to them; he also wanted a style that was uniquely his own. He experimented, composed, then finally recorded. The first glimpse of the "new" Cat Stevens style of music was offered to the public via the album *Mona Bone Jakon* in 1970. It was a major success, from a critical standpoint as well as at the record store counters. And the very singular style of Cat Stevens was fully established.

By 1971, Stevens was as popular in the United States as he was in Europe. A national tour and broad television exposure contributed to the recognition he was experiencing and a steady stream of top-selling albums and singles reinforced it. *Mona Bone Jakon*, showcase of his new style, was accepted well enough in America to earn a gold certification.

In regard to his illness, Stevens later said: "In its own way, it was the best thing that ever happened to me. I just couldn't go on doing the kind of music I'd done before it. It gave me the time to sit back and assess just what I needed to do to get the good music out of mind and into reality."

It did indeed happen. *Mona Bone Jakon* was only the first of a long line of certified gold albums. The appreciation came, of course, in the form of sales, but his work was also critically lauded, and Cat Stevens, the pop personality of the 60s was now respected as an introspective, lyrical rock artist of the 70s. The uniqueness that he had strived for had been achieved.

Rod Stewart

Scorecard

Platinum Albums — 3
Gold Albums — 8
Gold Singles — 3

Top Albums

The Rod Stewart Album (1969)
Gasoline Alley (1970)
*Every Picture Tells a Story** (1971)
*Never a Dull Moment** (1972)
*Sing It Again Rod** (1973)
Smiler (1974)
*Atlantic Crossing** (1975)
*The Best of Rod Stewart** (1976)
*A Night on the Town** (1976)
The Best of Rod Stewart, Vol. 2 (1976)
*Foot Loose and Fancy Free*** (1977)
*Blondes Have More Fun*** (1978)

Memorable Singles

Street Fighting Man (1969)
Handbags and Gladrags (1970)
Gasoline Alley (1970)
Dirty Old Town (1971)
*Maggie May** (1971)
Mandolin Wind (1971)
You Wear It Well (1972)
Twistin' the Night Away (1973)
Oh! No, Not My Baby (1973)
Farewell (1974)
Sailor (1975)
Let Me Be Your Car (1975)
Sailing (1975)
This Old Heart of Mine (1975)
*Tonight's the Night** (1976)
Hard Road (1976)
Sweet Little Rock n' Roller (1976)
The First Cut Is the Deepest (1977)
*You're in My Heart** (1978)
Do You Think I'm Sexy (1978)

Current Recording Label: Warner Bros.

** Platinum Certification
 * Gold Certification

The story, as it's been told, has it that Rod Stewart back in 1964 was singing a blues song aloud as he waited in the Twickenham Station in London for a late train home one night. In the nearby empty terminal another would-be commuter, Long John Baldry, heard him singing. Baldry, who was in the process of putting together a rock group, which he was calling the Hoochie Coochie Men, on the strength alone of the unintended audition, asked young Stewart to join his group as a second vocalist. So the story goes anyway.

Long John Baldry, a singer-songwriter himself, certainly did have an eye and an ear for talent (several years later he would also adopt another protege and help him get started — Elton John). How Long John and Rod Stewart came together doesn't really matter, the fact that they did, however, proved to be an important career stepping-stone for Stewart. As one writer put it, "The years with Baldry were crucial to Rod's musical evolution."

That evolution was enacted over a period that extended from 1961 through 1971. Through those years, Stewart served a rock apprenticeship by playing with a number of groups, the Hoochie Coochie Men was just one of them. The others included Jimmy Powell and the Dimensions (while Stewart was a harmonica-playing teenager), the Steampacket Band, the Shotgun Express (which was guided by Mick Fleetwood and Peter Green before they founded Fleetwood Mac), the Jeff Beck Group, and lastly Faces.

Rod Stewart, born in Scotland in the last months of World War II but raised in London, had wanted to be a rock singer and musician from the days of his early teens. He did try his hand briefly at other things, including a stint with a professional soccer team, the Brentford Football Club. But none of it was as appealing to him as music. At the very beginning, he struck out on a vagabond tour of continental Europe, an amateur minstrel singing and playing the guitar. Then he returned to London and worked with the various groups that were so much a part of his first professional decade in the rock business.

1971 was the year that Rod Stewart went solo. It was the year that his single *Maggie May* and the album *Every Picture Tells A Story* were released and soared to the top of the Charts both in England and the United States. After that, he continued to work with Faces as a group but at the same time did quite a bit of solo work on another record label. His total break with Faces did not become a reality until 1975. A year after that, however, he turned around and formed his own group to serve as a back-up both on stage and in the studio and also, as he described it, "to be a source of ideas and inspiration."

During the 1970s, Rod Stewart has become one of the world's premier rock male vocalists. It has not been easy, especially those days back in the early 1960s but, as Stewart readily admits, it's a lot less bruising and more fulfilling than playing soccer for a living.

Barbra Streisand

Scorecard

Platinum Albums — 4
Gold Albums — 22
Gold Singles — 3
Grammy Awards — 6

Top Albums

I Can Get It for You Wholesale (1962)
(original cast)
*The Barbra Streisand Album** (1963)
*The Second Barbra Streisand Album**
(1963)
*The Third Album** (1963)
Funny Girl (original cast)* (1964)
*People** (1964)
*My Name is Barbra** (1965)
*My Name is Barbra, Two** (1965)
*Color Me Barbra** (1966)
Je M'Appelle Barbra (1966)
Simply Streisand (1966)
*A Christmas Album** (1967)
A Happening in Central Park (1968)
Funny Girl (soundtrack) (1968)
What About Today (1969)
Hello Dolly (soundtrack) (1969)
*Barbra Streisand's Greatest Hits** (1970)
On a Clear Day You Can See Forever
(soundtrack) (1970)
The Owl and the Pussycat (soundtrack)
(1971)
*Stoney End** (1971)
*Barbra Joan Streisand** (1971)
*Live Concert at the Forum** (1972)
*Barbra Streisand . . . And Other Musical
Instruments* (1973)
*The Way We Were** (1973)
The Way We Were (soundtrack)* (1973)
*Butterfly** (1974)
Funny Lady (soundtrack)* (1975)
*Lazy Afternoon** (1976)
A Star Is Born (soundtrack)** (1976)
*Streisand Superman** (1977)
*Songbird*** (1978)
Eyes of Laura Mars (soundtrack) (1978)
*Greatest Hits, Vol. 2*** (1978)

Memorable Singles

*The Way We Were** (1974)
*Love Theme from a Star Is Born** (1976)
*You Don't Bring Me Flowers Anymore**
(1978)

Grammy Awards

1963 Album of the Year: *The Barbra
Streisand Album*
Best Pop Vocal Performance,
Female: *The Barbra Streisand
Album*
1964 Best Pop Vocal Performance,
Female: *People*
1965 Best Pop Vocal Performance,
Female: *My Name is Barbra*
1977 Song of the Year: *Love Theme
from a Star Is Born*
Best Pop Vocal Performance:
Love Theme from A Star Is Born

Current Recording Label: Columbia

** Platinum Certification
* Gold Certification

Barbra Streisand has a platform all her own in the topmost level of stardom. Since the early 1960s, she has been a unique, thoroughly individual performer, a superstar who first conquered the medium of recorded music, then television, the Broadway stage, and finally pictures.

Today, just as they were in 1963, her records are always found at or near the top of the Charts, sustaining an incredible string of hits that has been equalled by very few performers. And today, too, she is regarded as one of the very few "bankable" movie stars, whose simple presence on the screen virtually assures a box office success.

Born in Brooklyn, she spent all her school-age years in the New York metropolitan area before invading the American consciousness in 1963 with her first solo album, simply entitled *The Barbra Streisand Album.* It moved directly up the Charts, eventually earning a gold certification, and reaping two Grammy awards for her that year. *Cue* magazine named her Entertainer of the Year, and Barbra Streisand was suddenly a certified superstar.

By the mid-1960s, Barbra Streisand was one of the most sought after talents for television where she appeared on various specials and variety shows. From 1965 through 1968, she starred in a major TV special each year, all four of which were blazing successes. And each of those years she had also dominated the Charts with her albums and singles. The awards rolled in: more Grammies; an Emmy for her TV special, *My Name Is Barbra;* honors from *Playboy* magazine, *Mademoiselle,* and a host of other publications.

In 1968, Barbra Streisand took on Hollywood. Her first role was a starring one, the part of Fanny Brice in the musical comedy *Funny Girl,* the same role she had played on Broadway. Her debut was outstanding enough to win her the Oscar that year for Best Actress. Since that time she has made a motion picture every one of the ensuing 12 years, with only three exceptions — 1971, 1977, and 1978. Two songs she made famous in those movies also were awarded Oscars: *The Way We Were* in 1973 and *The Love Theme from A Star Is Born* in 1977.

It all began for her with a small production off-Broadway back in 1961. The show was *Another Evening with Harry Stoones* and it was Barbra Streisand's first professional role. The following year, she made it to Broadway with a supporting role in the musical *I Can Get It For You Wholesale,* for which the New York Drama Critics Poll honored her as Best Supporting Actress that year. From there, it was simply a matter of getting her first solo album down on vinyl and into the hands of America's record store owners; the public was out there waiting for her.

Barbra Streisand has reached that lofty height of success that only a few have managed to ascend to — Frank Sinatra, Judy Garland, Ella Fitzgerald, the Beatles, there are not many more. And for her, it was an incredibly short, swift journey from anonymity in Brooklyn to worldwide acclaim.

Styx

Scorecard

Platinum Albums — 2
Gold Albums — 4

Top Albums

Styx I (1970)
*Styx II** (1972)
The Serpent Is Rising (1973)
Man of Miracles (1974)
*Equinox** (1975)
Crystal Ball (1976)
*The Grand Illusion*** (1977)
*Pieces of Eight*** (1978)

Memorable Singles

Lady (1972)
Come Sail Away (1977)
Renegade (1978)
Sing for the Day (1978)

Current Recording Label: A & M
  Records

** Platinum Certification
 * Gold Certification

Chuck Panozzo — *Bass Guitar*   Dennis De Young — *Accordion*
John Panozzo — *Drums*   James Young — *Guitar*

Styx has been in the business of Rock for a long time. But most of it was spent in lonely anonymity as they moved from club to club and school gymnasium to coffeehouse in Chicago and its environs where they served their long apprenticeship.

Styx actually goes all the way back to 1963, even though they had a different name then and the group was only a trio composed of three young teenagers, the Panozzo brothers and Dennis De Young.

In 1968, they expanded. Guitarists James Young and John Curulewski joined with the three, and the new group christened themselves the Tradewinds. They began creating their own material around the same time, and it proved to be good enough to eventually earn them a shot at recording. Wooden Nickel Records, a subsidiary of RCA that distributed locally in the midwest, agreed to handle their first album. For it, the Tradewinds changed their name to Styx, and their first album was optimistically entitled Styx I.

The year was 1970, but Styx was a long way from making themselves known outside the American midwest. Wooden Nickel, however, was pleased enough with their output to sponsor three subsequent albums that Styx produced during the next five years. Then, after their fifth album was released, a strange kind of thing happened, not at all characteristic of other success stories in Rock annals. One of the songs from their second album, introduced years earlier, suddenly began to get a good amount of air play on the radio. *Lady* was the song, and its popularity spread so far that it revived interest in the album and sent the sales of it soaring up over 500,000 copies.

With a sudden respectability of their status in hand, Styx signed on with A & M Records for their next album. They did it, however, without John Curulewski, who left the group and was replaced by Tommy Shaw. The new album, *Equinox,* was a dazzling success, first in Canada and then in the United States. And Styx had reached full-fledged star quality — at least in North America.

The following year, the group set out on a 200-stop tour, and personally introduced themselves to the millions of people who had now become their fans and who were buying up their records in the U.S., Canada, and now many other parts of the world as well.

Each album since *Equinox* back in 1975 has been a major hit. Styx has become one of the hottest items in the business, known now throughout the world for the quality of the music they create as well as the surrealism of the album art that accompanies their records and their "extraordinary traveling shows," as their performances were called by one Rock writer. It took a long time, and James Young summed it up succinctly but aptly when he said: "We worked for our success."

Jethro Tull

Scorecard

Platinum Albums — 1
Gold Albums — 12

Top Albums

This Was (1969)
*Stand Up** (1969)
*Benefit** (1970)
*Aqualung** (1971)
*Thick as a Brick** (1972)
*Living in the Past** (1972)
*A Passion Play** (1973)
*War Child** (1974)
*M.U. The Best of Jethro Tull*** (1975)
*Minstrel in the Gallery** (1975)
Too Old to Rock and Roll, Too Young to Die (1976)
Jethro Tull (1976)
*Songs from the Wood** (1977)
Repeat: The Best of Jethro Tull, Vol. 2 (1977)
*Heavy Horses** (1978)
*Bursting Out** (1978)

Memorable Singles

The Witch's Promise (1970)
Inside (1970)
Hymn 24 (1971)
Hymn 43 (1971)
Locomotive Breath (1971)
Living in the Past (1972)
Passion Play Edit — 8 (1973)
Bungle in the Jungle (1974)
Skating Away (1974)
Minstrel in the Gallery (1975)
Too Old to Rock and Roll, Too Young to Die (1976)

Current Recording Label: Chrysalis

** Platinum Certification
 * Gold Certification

Ian Anderson — *Vocals, Flute, Guitar*
Martin Barre — *Guitar*
John Evan — *Keyboards*
David Palmer — *Keyboards*
John Glascock — *Bass*
Barriemore Barlow — *Drums*

In the 1700s, Jethro Tull was a British agriculturist who invented the mechanical crop drill and wrote a book about his work, entitled *The New Horses Hoeing Husbandry.* In the late 1960s and 70s, Jethro Tull is a British rock group that launched itself in Blackpool, an English resort city on the Irish Sea just up from Liverpool, who decided for one reason or another to adopt the agriculturist's name for their very own.

Ian Anderson is today the only member of the original four-man group that was formed back in 1967 as Jethro Tull. The other present-day members joined the group during the years 1968 through 1971.

In 1968, Anderson brought Jethro Tull down to London with the hope of expanding the group's horizon beyond merely performing for the vacationing crowds at Blackpool. What he brought was his own original approach to performing rock, as frenetic perhaps as any in those uninhibited and experimental days of British rock in the late 1960s.

Wildest of the group was founder and flute-player Ian Anderson, who would play his instrument while leaping in the air, groveling on his knees, lying on his back, or standing on one leg with the other perched flamingo-style. The music that he and the group produced, aptly called progressive rock, was never, however, subordinated to their antics on stage. The music is distinct, original and, as one writer referred to it: "Well-played, well-constructed, well-executed phantasmagoric views of the old versus the new."

Jethro Tull actually made it big only a little more than a year after Ian Anderson started the group. They were an instant success at the Sunbury Jazz and Blues Festival, a national rock event in England, when they debuted there in 1968. The following year, the group cut its first album, *This Was,* which scored exceptionally well in England. Its export to the United States was aided by Jethro Tull's first tour of the U.S.

From that point on, the name Jethro Tull established itself alongside all the other major rock groups that would dominate the 1970s. The energizing, frantic machinations on the stages of the world have made them one of the most popular live-performing groups in the business. Today, they tour regularly (usually twice a year nationally in the U.S. and once a year in Europe). With music that ranges from lyrical ballads to rock freak-outs, there are very few groups today who can captivate an audience in quite the same way as Jethro Tull.

The Who

Roger Daltry — *Vocals*
Pete Townshend — *Guitar*

Keith Moon — *Drums*
John Entwistle — *Bass*

The Who could never be called your ordinary, run of the mill young men. Singer Roger Daltry often appeared on stage with a safety pin impaled through one of his nostrils. Pete Townshend would frequently end a performance by ramming the neck of his guitar into the amplifier until the guitar shattered. Off-stage, too. Keith Moon, the story goes, was reportedly arrested for trying to water petunias of his Los Angeles neighbor Steve McQueen with brandy, naked. John Entwistle, it is said, just puts up with it all.

The Who, precursors of "Punk Rock," have been described with adjectives that have ranged from hyperkinetic to insane. All of them, at one time or another, have probably been appropriate. Even when money was hard to come by for the group, they would often destroy all their instruments in the climax of a performance.

It all began back in a working class section of London called Shepherd's Bush in the late 1950s. Pete Townshend and John Entwistle, still in high school and playing with a traditional Dixieland band, joined with Roger Daltry to form a new mod-rock group. They called themselves the Detours. Several other members came and went as the group played its way through various local pubs in London.

By 1963, they felt they were ready for professional management, so they hired Helmut Gordon, a doorknob maker, to handle their affairs. Then they signed Keith Moon as drummer when in a public audition he showed his zeal for the job by beating the drums into total destruction. They changed their name to the High Numbers, which they kept for a year, and then discarded it in favor of The Who.

My Generation was The Who's first solid hit, issued in November 1965. It also became the title song of their first album, which was released five months later.

The more they worked together, the stranger their antics on stage — characterized by wild leaps in the air, screaming, various and sundry forms of violence to their instruments, clothes, even the stage itself. They were looked upon as an oddity by many, but by 1967 they had become a cult image, their popularity fueled by the release that year of the moody, deeply introspective single *I Can See for Miles*. They followed that with the rock opera *Tommy* in 1969, and the message quickly spread that despite their eccentric behavior The Who were not only very serious musicians but rock innovators as well. *Tommy* was called by one writer, "the finest extended thematic structure any rock group ever pulled off."

Since those days, the group has split, then reformed, and the individuals within it have on occasion struck out on their own. As a group today, The Who is a legend in the rock world. And the stage antics may be a bit subdued now, at least comparatively speaking, but the act's still a strange blend of madness and talent.

Scorecard

Platinum Albums — 1
Gold Albums — 8

Top Albums

My Generation (1966)
Happy Jack (1967)
The Who Sell Out (1967)
Magic Bus (1968)
Tommy* (1969)
The Who Live at Leeds* (1970)
Who's Next* (1971)
Meaty, Beaty, Big and Bouncy* (1971)
Quadrophenia* (1973)
Odds and Sods* (1974)
A Quick One . . .* (1974)
Magic Bus . . . (1974)
The Who by Numbers* (1975)
Who Are You** (1978)

Memorable Singles

I Can't Explain (1964)
Anyway, Anyhow, Anywhere (1965)
My Generation (1965)
The Kids Are Alright (1966)
I'm a Boy (1966)
I Can See for Miles (1967)
Call Me Lightning (1968)
Magic Bus (1968)
Pinball Wizard (1969)
I'm Free (1969)
The Seeker (1970)
Summertime Blues (1970)
See Me, Feel Me (1970)
Overture from Tommy (1970)
Won't Get Fooled Again (1971)
My Wife (1971)
Join Together (1972)
Wasp Man (1972)
Love, Reign O'er Me (1973)
The Real Me (1974)
Postcard (1974)
Squeeze Box (1975)
Slip Kid (1976)

Current Recording Label: MCA Records

** Platinum Certification
* Gold Certification

Scorecard

Gold Albums — 5
Gold Singles — 18
Grammy Awards — 14

Top Albums

12-Year-Old Genius (1963)
Greatest Hits (1968)
For Once in My Life (1968)
My Cherie Amour (1969)
Greatest Hits, Vol.2 (1971)
*Music of My Mind** (1972)
*Talking Book** (1972)
*Innervisions** (1973)
*Fulfillingness's First Finale** (1974)
*Songs in the Key of Life** (1976)
Looking Back (1977)

Memorable Singles

*Fingertips** (1973)
*Uptight** (1965)
*I Was Made to Love Her** (1967)
*For Once in My Life** (1968)
*My Cherie Amour** (1969)
*Yester-Me, Yester-You, Yesterday** (1969)
*Signed, Sealed and Delivered** (1970)
*Heaven Help Us All** (1970)
*If You Really Love Me** (1971)
*Super Woman** (1972)
*Superstition** (1972)
*Higher Ground** (1973)
*You Are the Sunshine of My Life** (1973)
*Living for the City** (1973)
*You Haven't Done Nothin'** (1974)
*Boogie on Reggae Woman** (1974)
*Don't You Worry About a Thing** (1974)
*I Wish** (1977)

Grammy Awards

1973 Album of the Year: *Innervisions*
 Best Pop Vocal, Male: *You Are the Sunshine of My Life*
 Best Rhythm & Blues, Male: *Superstition*
 Best Rhythm & Blues Song: *Superstition*
 Best Engineered Recording: *Innervisions*
1974 Album of the Year: *Fulfillingness's First Finale*
 Album of the Year, Producer: *Fulfillingness's First Finale*
 Best Pop Vocalist, Male: *Fulfillingness's First Finale*
 Best Rhythm & Blues, Males: *Boogie on Reggae Woman*
 Best Rhythm & Blues Song: *Living for the City*
1976 Album of the Year: *Songs in the Key of Life*
 Best Producer of the Year: *Songs in the Key of Life*
 Best Pop Vocalist, Male: *Songs in Key of Life*
 Best Rhythm & Blues, Male: *I Wish*

Current Recording Label: Motown

* Gold Certification

Stevie Wonder

Steveland Morris was born blind in Saginaw, Michigan, back in 1951. At two years old, like most ordinary children, he took to toys, even flailing away at a set of tin drums from time to time. At three, however, the similarity with other youngsters ended somewhat abruptly. Steveland took up playing the piano at that age. Not too long after that he taught himself to play the harmonica, a simple four-hole model of that instrument. He did it by learning to play along with the blues songs he listened to on the radio. His voice was also melodic and he was enlisted to sing at the Whitestone Baptist Church in Detroit. Everybody who knew him or heard him sing or perform said he was a child prodigy, a young genius is the way most of them put it.

At the age of 10, Steveland was introduced to some people at Motown Records. They, too, agreed he was something special. They suggested he change his name to "Little" Stevie Wonder and record with them. By the age 12, Little Stevie had a Top-10 Single and a national hit album on the Motown label. His first album was appropriately entitled *12-Year-Old Genius*.

A tutor worked with him in those days when he was not recording, rehearsing, performing live, or touring; and besides the language arts, math, and other basic school subjects for a youngster he was also studying musical theory, composition, and interpretation.

Stevie Wonder, a prodigious talent despite his blindness, was that rare phenomenon in the music world — a smash success right from the very beginning. He served no real apprenticeship as so many other recording artists have had to. All of it came as easy to him as walking or talking might to another youngster.

The hits came one after the other. His discography reads like a Hall of Fame of rock music during the late 1960s and the 70s. He was on the road most of the time when other teenagers were spending their days inside a high school classroom. His travels took him from night clubs to college campuses and vast outdoor stadiums, from small towns in the United States to national capitals throughout the world.

It came very close to ending for him, however, in the summer of 1973. The car he was riding in crashed head-on into a logging truck on a highway just outside Durham, North Carolina. The young singer was in a coma afterwards, near death the doctors said, but he came out of it and after a seven-month convalescence was back at his profession.

When the Grammy awards for 1973 were announced, he won his first *five* in that single year. It was an incredible accomplishment for a 22-year-old. It was, of course, just the beginning of a long line of major awards he would win. No single entertainer, male or female, in fact, has posted a record of achievement awards in recent years that can compare to what has been bestowed on Stevie Wonder.

Yes

Jon Anderson — *Vocals*
Chris Squire — *Vocals, Bass*
Steve Howe — *Guitar*

Patrick Moraz — *Keyboards*
Alan White — *Drums*

Scorecard

Platinum Albums — 1
Gold Albums — 8

Top Albums

Yes (1969)
Time and a Word (1970)
The Yes Album* (1971)
Fragile* (1972)
Close to the Edge* (1972)
Yessongs* (1973)
Tales from Topographic Oceans* (1974)
Relayer* (1974)
Yesterdays (1975)
Going for the One* (1977)
Tormato** (1978)

Memorable Singles

Sweetness (1970)
Your Move (1971)
Roundabout (1972)
America (1972)
And You and I (1972)
Soon (1975)
Wonderous Stories (1977)

Solo Albums

Beginnings (Steve Howe) (1975)
Fish Out of Water (Chris Squire) (1975)
Ramshackled (Alan White) (1976)
i (Patrick Moraz) (1976)
Olias of Sunhillow (Jon Anderson) (1976)

Solo Singles

Lucky Seven (Chris Squire) (1976)
Oooh Baby (Alan White) (1976)
Flight of the Moorglade (Jon Anderson) (1976)

Current Recording Label: Atlantic

** Platinum Certification
 * Gold Certification

Only two members remain from the original Yes, which was begun back in 1968; the same two who sat at a bar in a Soho club in London one night that year and kicked around the idea of forming their own group, Jon Anderson and Chris Squire. The kind of music they wanted to put together was, as Jon Anderson's describes it, "a kind of folk-pop-rock-classical continuum."

Finding the right people to fill out their group, those with similar interests and aims, was a definite problem. But they solved it by recruiting Peter Banks (guitar), Bill Bruford (drums), and Tony Kaye (keyboards). Then they needed a name for the group: "For the kind of music we were contemplating," Anderson said later, "we had to have a strong and straight title for the band." Nothing is perhaps more direct or positive than a simple "Yes," they decided.

The group began working various small clubs in London. Then two big breaks came back-to-back. In October 1968, they were asked to fill in at a major club, The Speakeasy, for Sly and the Family Stone, who had backed out at the last moment. Two months later and partly as a result of their fine acceptance at the Speakeasy, they were signed to open the farewell concert of Cream (with Eric Clapton) at Royal Albert Hall. They did and were a smash hit before a packed house of more than 10,000 that night.

It was enough to enable Yes to get its first album down on vinyl. It was not, however, until 1971 before the group could claim any really serious following in England, and not for a year after that until their name became sufficiently known in America.

The Yes Album, their third LP, rose to the top of the English charts in early 1971, followed by the single *Your Move* a few months later. The group toured the United States that year to promote the new records, but it wasn't actually until the following year and the release of the single *Roundabout* that they could truthfully say they had successfully crossed the Atlantic and been discovered in the New World.

Since those days, the faces of Yes have changed. Peter Banks left in 1970 to form his own group called Flash and Steve Howe replaced him on guitar. The following year, Rick Wakeman came over from Strawbs to fill in for Tony Kaye (and was himself replaced in 1974 by Patrick Moraz). Bill Bruford then left to join King Crimson and Alan White took his place at the drums. All five of the present members of Yes have since cut solo albums apart from their work as a group.

Despite the changes in personnel over the years and the individuality of each performer, Yes, with their majestical, complex, and rewarding form of Pop/Rock music, has consistently been well-received. As one writer put it: "They have never had to look back, but only move forward in the process of creating and refining *Yes* music."

PHOTO CREDITS

Without the assistance of fourteen of the top rock and pop recording companies of the world, the information and photographs included in this book would have been impossible to compile. The author and publisher of *Rock Stars: People at the Top of the Charts* are deeply indebted to the following companies who were kind enough to supply photographs of their greatest stars for inclusion in this book.

A&M Records, New York, N.Y.: pages 42, 43, (Bandana Mdse. Inc.), 76, 77, 82, 83.

Arista Records, New York, NY: 58 (Jay Thompson), 59 (Lee Gurst).

Asylum Records, Los Angeles, CA: 18, 19, 67 (Jim Shea).

Atlantic Recording Corp., New York, NY: 36, 37, 40, 41, 45, 65, 90, 91.

Capitol Records, Inc. Hollywood, CA: 55, 61 (Clive Arrowsmith), 73.

Casablanca Records and FilmWorks, Los Angeles, CA: 57 (Au Coin Management, Inc.).

Chrysalis Records, Los Angeles, CA: 85

Columbia Records, New York, NY: 13 (Ron Pownall), 23, 31, 49, 71, 81.

Elektra Records, Los Angeles, CA: 75 (Eric Meola).

Epic Records, New York, NY: 17 (Ron Pownall), 53.

MCA Records, Universal City, CA: 50, 51, 63, 86, 87.

Motown, Hollywood, CA: 27, 29.

RSO Records, Los Angeles, CA: 15, 25, 47.

Warner Bros. Records, Burbank, CA: 28, 29, 32, 33, 38, 39, 68, 69, 78, 79.

Title Page photo montage. *Top row, left to right:* Rod Stewart: Warner Bros. Records; Maurice Gibb: RSO Records, Inc.; Robin Gibb: RSO Records, Inc.; Carly Simon: Elektra Records. *Bottom Row, left to right:* Keith Moon: MCA Records; Olivia Newtown-John: MCA Records; Rolling Stones members: Atlantic Records; Mick Jagger, Atlantic Records; The Captain & Tennille: A&M Records; Ian Anderson of Jethro Tull: Chrysalis Records.

Photo montage on p. 11. *Top:* Al Greenwood, Mick Jones and Lou Gramm of Foreigner: Atlantic Records. *Middle row, left to right:* Linda Ronstadt: Asylum Records (Jim Shea); Pete Townshend of The Who: MCA Records; Roger Daltrey of The Who: MCA Records. *Bottom:* Alice Cooper and friend: Warner Bros. Records.

Photo montage on pp. 92 & 93. *Top row, left to right:* Bee Gees: RSO Records; Alice Cooper: Warner/Reprise; Andy Gibb: RSO Records. *Bottom row, left to right:* Linda McCartney: Capitol Records; Todd Rundgren: Warner Bros. Records; Elton John: MCA Records (Terry O'Neill); Carly Simon: Elektra Records.

Index

A

A&M Records, 20, 42, 76, 82
Abbott, Drew, 72
Aerosmith, 12
Allman Brothers, 9
America, 18
American Dream, 68
American Legion, 22
Anderson, Ian, 84
Anderson, Jon, 90
Aristo Records, 58
Association, the, 9
Asylum Records, 66
Atlantic Records, 36, 40, 44, 90
Avatar, 54

B

Baez, Joan, 18
Bailey, Philip, 34
Baker, Ginger, 24
Baldry, Long John, 50, 78
Bang Records, 30
Banks, Peter, 90
Barlow, Barriemore, 84
Barre, Martin, 84
Basie, Count, 44
Baxter, Jeff, 32
Beach Boys, 8, 20
Beatles, the, 8, 60, 80
Bee Gees, the, 14, 26, 46
Billboard magazine, 10, 14, 26, 28, 32, 44, 62
Blind Faith, 24
Blood, Sweat & Tears, 9, 54
Bluesbreakers, John Mayall's, 24
Bluesology, 50
Boone, Debby, 10
Boston, 16, 26
Bowie, David, 10
Bridges, Alicia, 10
Browne, Jackson, 16
Bruce, Jack, 24
Bruford, Bill, 90
Buckingham, Lindsey, 38
Butterfield, Paul, 68

C

Campbell, Chris, 72
Capitol Records, 54, 60, 72
Captain & Tennille, the, 20
Carnegie Hall, 48
Carpenters, the, 9
Carroll, Pat, 62
Cars, the, 10
Casablanca, 56
Cash Box, 10, 22, 44, 62
CBS, 58
Cetera, Peter, 22
Charles, Ray, 8
Checker, Chubby, 48
Chic, 10
Chicago, 22
Chicago Conservatory of Music, 34
Chickenshack, 38
Chrysalis Records, 84
City, the, 54
Clapton, Eric, 24, 90
Cocker, Joe, 9, 18

Columbia Records, 12, 22, 30, 34, 44, 48, 70, 80
Commodores, the, 26
Como, Perry, 7
Cooper, Alice, 28
Cream, 9, 24, 90
Credence Clearwater Revival, 9
Criss, Peter, 56
Cue, 80
Curulewski, John 82

D

Dacus, Donnie, 22
Daltry, Roger, 86
Delaney & Bonnie, 24
Delp, Brad, 16
Denver, John, 10
Derek and the Dominoes, 24
Detours, the, 86
De Young, Dennis, 82
Diamond, Neil, 30, 54
Domino, Fats, 8
Doobie Brothers, 32
Doors, the, 9
Dragon, Daryl, 20
Drifters, the, 54
Dunn, Larry, 34
Dylan, Bob, 9

E

Eagles, the, 10, 18, 66
Earth, Wind & Fire, 34
Earwigs, 28
Edwards, Kenny, 66
Ehart, Phil, 52
Elektra Records, 74
Elliot, Dennis, 40
Emerson, Keith, 36
Emerson, Lake & Palmer, 36
Emmy Awards, 58, 80
Entwistle, John, 42, 86
Epic, 16, 52
Escoveda, Pete, 70
Evan, John, 84
Everly Brothers, the, 8

F

Faces, 78
Fifth Dimension, the, 9
Fitzgerald, Ella, 80
Flack, Roberta, 9
Flash, 90
Fleetwood Mac, 38, 78
Foreigner, 26, 40
Frampton, Peter, 42
Franklin, Aretha, 9, 44, 54
Frehley, Ace, 56
Frey, Glenn, 66

G

Gagliardi, Ed, 40
Gallup Poll, 10, 26
Garland, Judy, 80
Gibb, Andy, 46
Gilder, Nick, 10

Glascock, John, 84
Godspell, 9
Goffin, Gerry, 54
Goudreau, Barry, 16
Graham, Johnny, 34
Gramm, Lou, 40
Grammy Awards, 7, 8, 9, 14, 20, 30, 34, 38, 44, 46, 54, 58, 60, 66, 74, 80, 88
Grand Funk Railroad, 10, 68
Grateful Dead, the, 9
Grease, 62
Greenwood, Al, 40

H

Hair, 9
Haley, Bill, 8
Hamilton, Tom, 12
Hammond, John, 44
Harrison, George, 42
Hartman, John, 32
Hashian, Sib, 16
Heatwave, 10
Hendrix, Jimi, 9
Henley, Don, 66
Hell's Angels, 64
Herd, 42
Herman's Hermits, 8-9
Holiday, Billie, 44
Holly, Buddy, 8
Hoochie Coochie Men, 78
Hope, Dave, 52
Hossack, Michael, 32
Howe, Steve, 90
Humble Pie, 42
Humperdinck, Englebert, 9

J

Jackson 5, the, 18
Jagger, Mick, 64
James, Rick, 10
Jeff Beck Group, 78
Jennings, Waylon, 7
Jesus Christ Superstar, 9
Jethro Tull, 84
Joel, Billy, 48
John, Elton, 50, 62, 78
Johnson, Ralph, 34
Johnston, Tom, 32
Jones, Brian, 64
Jones, Mick, 40
Joplin, Janis, 9

K

Kansas, 52
Kaye, Tony, 90
Kimmel, Bob, 66
King, Carole, 54
King Crimson, 36
King, William, 26
Kirschner, Don, 52
Kirwan, Danny, 38
Kiss, 26, 56
Knight, Gladys & the Pips, 9
Knights of Columbus, 16
Knudsen, Keith, 32
Kortchmar, Danny, 54

Kramer, Jerry, 12
Kristoferson, Kris, 9, 74

L

Laine, Denny, 60
Lake, Greg, 36
Lamm, Robert, 22
LaPread, Ronald, 26
Larkey, Charles, 54
Lear, Graham, 70
Leber-Krebs, Inc., 12
Led Zeppelin, 9
Lewis, Jerry Lee, 8
Lewis, Ramsey, 34
Lincoln Center, 48
Lindley, David, 18
Livgren, Kerry, 52
London, Laurie, 7
Loughnane, Lee, 22
Lynyrd Skynyrd, 10

M

Mancini, Henry, 7
Manilow, Barry, 58
Margen, David, 70
Marriot, Steve, 42
Martin, Steve, 7
Mathis, Johnny, 58
Mayall, John, 24, 38
MCA Records, 30, 50, 86
McCartney, Linda, 60
McCartney, Paul, & Wings, 60
McClary, Thomas, 26
McDonald, Ian, 40
McDonald, Michael, 32
McKay, Al, 34
McQueen, Steve, 86
McVie, John, 38
Meat Loaf, 10, 68
Memphis Backstreet Boys, 30
Middler, Bette, 9, 58
Mitchell, Joni, 10, 18
Modugno, Domenico, 7
Monkees, the, 9, 52
Moody Blues, the, 9
Moog synthesizer, 36
Moon, Keith, 86
Motown Records, 26, 88
Moraz, Patrick, 90
Mother Earth, 20

N

National Academy of Recording Arts and
    Sciences, 7
Nelson, Willie, 7
Newton, Wayne, 62
Newtown-John, Olivia, 46, 62
Nicks, Stevie, 38
Nitty Gritty Dirt Band, the, 18
Nilsson, Harry, 42
Noonan, Steve, 18
Nugent, Ted, 10, 12

O

Oliveira, Laudir de, 22
Orange, Walter Clyde, 26
Oscars (Academy Awards), 74, 80
Osmonds, the, 10

P

Palmer, Carl, 36
Palmer, David, 84
Pankow, James, 22
Panozzo, Chuck, 82
Panozzo, John, 82
Parazider, Walt, 22
Parton, Dolly, 7
Peraza, Armando, 70
Perry, Joe, 12
Porter, Tiran, 32
Powell, Jimmy, 78
Prado, Perez, 7
Presley, Elvis, 7, 8, 30
Pud, 32

Q

Queen, 10

R

Rafferty, Gerry, 10
Raitt, Bonnie, 18
Record Industry Association of America, 7
Redding, Otis, 9
Reddy, Helen, 9
Reed, Alto, 72
Rekow, Raul, 70
Revere, Paul, and the Raiders, 9
Rhyne, Chris, 70
Richie, Lionel, 26
Richard, Keith, 64
Richard, Little, 8
Rivers, Johnny, 18
Robbins, Robyn, 72
Rolling Stone (magazine), 10, 44, 66
Rolling Stones, the, 8, 64
Rolling Stones Records, 64
Ronstadt, Linda, 18, 66
Royal Academy of Music, 50
RSO Records, 14, 24
Rundgren, Todd, 68

S

Santana, Carlos, 70
Saturday Night Fever, 14
Scholz, Tom, 16
Seger, Bob, 72
Seraphine, Danny, 22
Sheehan, Fran, 16
Shirelles, the, 54
Shogren, Dave, 32
Shotgun Express, 38
Simmons, Gene, 56
Simmons, Patrick, 32
Simon & Schuster, 74
Simon, Carly, 74
Sinatra, Frank, 30, 58, 80
Sly & the Family Stone, 9
Snow, Phoebe, 18
Solberg, Chris, 70
Sonny & Cher, 9
Spencer, Jeremy, 38
Spooky Tooth, 40
Squire, Chris, 90
Stanley, Paul, 56
Steely Dan, 32
Steinhardt, Robbie, 52
Stevens, Cat, 74, 76
Stewart, Rod, 38, 78

Stone Poneys, the, 66
Streisand, Barbra, 8, 30, 54, 80
Styx, 82
Summer, Donna, 26
Sunbury Jazz and Blues Festival, 84
Supremes, the, 8

T

Taste of Honey, A, 10
Taupin, Bernie, 50
Teegarden, David, 72
Tennille, Toni, 20
Three Dog Night, 9
Tommy, 86
Tony Awards, 58
Townshend, Pete, 86
Tradewinds, the, 82
Travolta, John, 62
Tyler, Bonnie, 10
Tyler, Steve, 12

U

Uni Records, 30
United Way, 32
Utopia, 68

V

Velvet Underground, 16
Village People, the, 10

W

Walker, Dave, 38
Walker, Greg, 70
Walsh, Steve, 52
Warner Bros. Records, 28, 38, 78
Watts, Charlie, 64
Welch, Bob, 10, 38
White, Alan, 90
White, Fred, 34
White, Maurice, 34
White, Verdine, 34
Whitford, Brad, 12
Who, the, 86
Williams, Millan, 26
Williams, Rich, 52
Wilson, Teddy, 44
Wonder, Stevie, 88
Wood, Ron, 64
Wooden Nickel Records, 82
Woodstock, 70
Woody's Truckstop, 68
Woolfolk, Andrew, 34
Wyman, Bill, 64

Y

Yardbirds, the, 24
Yes, 90
Young, James, 82
Young, Neil, 9